COPING WITH
AGGRESSIVE BEHAVIOUR

Glynis M. Breakwell

Personal and Professional Development

COPING WITH
AGGRESSIVE BEHAVIOUR

Glynis M. Breakwell

Social Psychology European Research Institute,
University of Surrey

BPS
BOOKS Published by The British Psychological Society

First published in 1997 by BPS Books (The British Psychological Society),
St Andrews House, 48 Princess Road East, Leicester LE1 7DR, UK.

A catalogue record for this book is available from the British Library.

ISBN 1 85433 205 8

Typeset by HouseStyle Graphics, Clerkenwell Road, London EC1M 5PS
Printed in Great Britain by Redwood Books, Trowbridge, Wilts.

Personal and Professional Development

SERIES EDITORS:
Glynis M. Breakwell is Professor of Psychology and Pro-Vice-Chancellor of the University of Surrey.

David Fontana is Reader in Educational Psychology at University of Wales College of Cardiff, and Professor Catedrático, University of Minho, Portugal.

The books in this series are designed to help readers use psychological insights, theories and methods to address issues which arise regularly in their own personal and professional lives and which affect how they manage their jobs and careers. Psychologists have a great deal to say about how to improve our work styles. The emphasis in this series is upon presenting psychology in a way which is easily understood and usable. We are committed to enabling our readers to use psychology, applying it for themselves to themselves.

The books adopt a highly practical approach. Readers are confronted with examples and exercises which require them to analyse their own situation and review carefully what they think, feel and do. Such analyses are necessary precursors in coming to an understanding of where and what changes are needed, or can reasonably be made.

These books do not reflect any single approach in psychology. The editors come from different branches of the discipline. They work together with the authors to ensure that each book provides a fair and comprehensive review of the psychology relevant to the issues discussed.

Each book deals with a clearly defined target and can stand alone. But combined they form an integrated and broad resource, making wide areas of psychological expertise more freely accessible.

IN MEMORY OF ELSIE ROWETT

1912–1995

Contents

Chapter One

Everybody Needs to Know
How to Cope with Aggression

Recently, a three-year-old gypsy boy and his 13-year-old sister were seriously injured when a booby-trapped doll, given to them by a passing motorist, exploded as they begged in the streets of Pisa, Italy. Not long after, a man walked into a primary school gymnasium in Dunblane, Scotland, armed with four handguns and opened fire on a class of five- and six-year-olds. Three minutes later all but one of the 29 children were wounded, dying or dead. Regular reports of 'ethnic cleansing', and other euphemisms for attempted genocide, emanate from Europe, Africa, Asia and South America as mass graves and burnt-out villages are discovered. Terrorists bomb inner-city areas, killing and maiming bystanders.

It is a violent world. We are surrounded by aggression and all of us have some personal experience of physical or emotional attacks. The media ensure that we have vivid vicarious experience of the violence perpetrated against others everywhere, and we are bombarded with details of young women stalked by obsessive, rejected suitors; of random sex attacks on the very old and very young; of 'road rage' victims chased along motorways, forced off the road and, on occasion, shot; of gangs of marauding drunks out of control in shopping centres; and details of every variety of family assault and domestic violence.

This is a book about aggression and how to cope with it. Everyone is capable of being aggressive and inflicting harm: each one of us has been guilty of violence at some time. To improve both our domestic and working lives, it is imperative that we learn how to cope more effectively with aggression and its consequences. Although the book is primarily directed at the caring professions – nurses, doctors, health visitors, teachers, social workers and others who attempt to offer advice, support, and skilled help, and who find themselves targeted for abuse and assault in the course of their work – the information in this book is useful for anyone who deals with other people, and we all do that. Violence is present in virtually all workplaces (Flannery, 1995) and we need to understand how to deal with it.

VIOLENCE AND THE CARING PROFESSIONS

The problem of aggression and physical violence is one of the most pressing concerns of members of the caring professions all over the world today. The force of the problem is highlighted by the growing number of fatal attacks upon carers and anyone in these professions will be aware of the sad catalogue of teachers shot or stabbed in their classrooms or school yards by pupils, the voluntary workers in hostels for the homeless or mentally ill strangled by inmates, the health visitors beaten to death in the homes of client families, the doctors and nurses knifed in their surgeries and hospitals by patients, the occupational therapists killed in psychiatric units, and the social workers stabbed, or sometimes abducted and tortured, by their clients.

Reports of attacks and injuries that are serious but not ultimately life-threatening are also readily available. For instance, there was the case of a social worker who was attacked with a meat cleaver by a client who had a history of psychiatric disturbance, and sustained serious injuries to her head and leg. In another incident, a 47-year-old social worker was raped, stabbed and robbed in her own office by a 17-year-old client. Such attacks are not restricted to female practitioners. A male GP has described how he was punched and kicked by a patient, resulting in a scrotal haematoma. Nor are such incidents restricted to the health and social services. In a survey of school teachers, one male respondent reported being attacked seven times over a period of 14 years: once with a knife, once with a stiletto, once with an air rifle, once when a pupil fed gas into his classroom while he was teaching, twice when pupils used their fists, and once when an ex-pupil tried to run him over with a car.

Carers are clearly at risk of abuse from the very people whom they are trying to help. This abuse is not always acute or easily visible; it is sometimes chronic but minor, and extends over long periods. For instance, many nurses will acknowledge the difficulties of bathtime on geriatric wards or in homes for the elderly. They are often bruised or scratched by confused or dementing patients attempting to escape the unwanted but needed assistance in keeping themselves clean. Other members of the caring professions will attest to the frequently severe challenging behaviour of some mentally disabled people.

Of course, abuse is not always physical. Sometimes it is embodied in verbal threats and accusations or other forms of harassment (for example, sexual innuendo used to embarrass or undermine authority). Aggression takes many forms, of which physical violence is only one. Any **deliberate** attempt to inflict harm, whether physically or psychologically, is an act of aggression. In practice, the problem with this definition lies in determining whether harm was actually deliberate or whether it was accidental; it is not aggressive to damage someone or something accidentally. Nevertheless, this is the most useful simple comprehensive definition of aggression that exists, and issues of definition will be discussed further later in this book. The essential point here is that, for the caring professions, aggression and violence are an integral part of the job: frightening, unacceptable but inevitable.

Over the last decade, carers have come to recognize that they must learn to care for themselves as well as their clients. In the context of the increased visibility of assaults and the real anxiety they provoke, we will look at the following questions.

THE IMPORTANT QUESTIONS

HOW DO SUCH ATTACKS OCCUR?

People want to know where and when violence is likely. They also want to know which sorts of people are most likely to be involved – who are the assaulted and who are the assailants? Do those who are attacked have a predictable profile of physical, psychological or professional characteristics that sets them apart? Is it possible to predict who will be aggressive?

WHY DO ATTACKS HAPPEN?

People want and need to understand why attacks happen – what goes wrong?; who should be held responsible?; what are the social and psychological processes that generate such violence and aggression?

This perceived need seems to be based on an assumption that explanation will lead to prevention. This assumption may be wrong;

explanation may facilitate prediction, but prevention is something quite different. Knowing the cause of an act of violence is only useful if, as a result, it is possible to remove the cause. For instance, the repetition of an incident where an elderly woman in a residential home becomes abusive because a male warden walks into her room without knocking, may be prevented by ensuring that the privacy and territoriality of residents are respected subsequently. However, many causes of violence are not so easy to alter. Violence can result from mental illness or from long-term economic deprivation, and such causes *cannot* be removed.

There is a further problem with the assumption that explanation can lead to control. Where specific acts of violence *can* be explained, it often turns out that several determinants have interacted to cause the incident. In practice, it is rarely possible to anticipate how determinants will interact such that they can be changed so as to avoid the eruption of violence.

This does not mean that explanations are pointless. Good explanations are the basis for prediction and anticipation; knowing what factors cause violence makes it possible to predict the circumstances under which it is likely to occur. Of course, the predictive powers of our explanations of violence are currently limited and are too general to allow good prediction in the specific case. Nevertheless, our explanations do take us some way to prediction and help to indicate what factors should concern us.

HOW SHOULD I COPE?

Carers want to know, first, how to avoid situations where attacks are likely and, secondly, how to deal with incidents when they do occur, including coping with their emotional and organizational aftermath.

WHAT ORGANIZATIONAL CHANGES WOULD HELP?

Employers have a legal obligation to provide for the safety of their employees. Consequently, most organizations want to know what they can do to reduce the possibility of any assault upon their staff. Changes can include modifications in selection, in training, in management procedures for dealing with practitioners at risk of being attacked or those who have been attacked, in the physical environment in the place of work or in communication systems. However, a big question mark still hangs over many of these possible management responses, as their efficacy and economic viability have not yet been established.

NO EASY ANSWERS

In an area of such public concern, where solutions are urgently required, it is important not to be deluded into thinking that any simple panaceas are on hand. Not all the questions can be answered currently. However, the object of this book is to try to provide some answers to the questions which have been outlined. I will draw upon a growing, if unsystematic, body of research, drawn often from the social services but also from the educational and health services. I will also use examples of 'good' practice from social service, health and education authorities where codes of practice and different patterns of resource provision have been introduced.

Understanding more about aggression can help you, whether you work in the caring professions or not, because knowledge helps to reduce unnecessary fear and empowers you to protect yourself and others.

ANALYSING THE PROBLEM

This book describes the most common sorts of incidents that happen and the ways in which they are treated. Typically, this will involve a description of what led up to the incident, the extent of the violence and its form, how the victim of the attack feels afterwards, reporting of incidents, management responses to them, the longer term effects of attacks, the stereotyping of the victim by other professionals and by management, and so on. This will be accompanied by a social psychological analysis (looking at the interaction between the individual and the social context) of the explanations for the violence and for the repercussions it has for practitioners attacked and for their employing organization. Case studies are used to illustrate the general points made.

TACTICS OF ANTICIPATION, AVOIDANCE AND ESCAPE

Tactics that the practitioner can use when faced with a potentially violent client will be described. These will not focus on techniques of physical self-defence or 'control and restraint' – this book is not a manual on self-defence. Instead, they will focus on the skills necessary to read the cues given by the client that an attack is likely and on the methods that can be employed to extricate oneself. Examples of ways that have been used by people in the past to get out of difficult situations will be discussed. These examples serve to emphasize that simple, general rules about how to behave in a violent situation cannot be formulated: in the light of the available information, **you** have to decide what strategies are likely to work for you.

THE AFTERMATH OF AN ATTACK

Common problems that carers experience after being involved in an attack are described, and methods which can be used to restore self-confidence, cope with self-doubt, and control guilt are considered. The 'double bind' situation which practitioners can be placed in by the demands of the job (that is, required to follow a caring philosophy yet required to control and constrain their clients) will be examined. The uneasy truce between these two conflicting sets of demands is shattered when the client becomes violent with the carer, and the whole fabric of the caring relationship is transformed. The questions are then: how does the practitioner carry on? how is the conception of the client changed? and how are relationships with colleagues altered?

PRACTITIONER VIOLENCE TOWARDS CLIENTS

In discussing violence against the practitioner, it would be inappropriate to ignore the violence that sometimes flows in the opposite direction – from the practitioner to the client. This has to be discussed as part of achieving an understanding of the dynamic of the 'caring' relationship. Powerful emotions are at work on both sides of the caring divide and they need to be recognized.

THE POSSIBILITY OF CHANGE

This is not a 'cookbook' on how to cope with violence exhibited by clients. Some suggestions on how to do that will inevitably be examined, but that is not the main aim. Instead, the book is aimed at helping you to understand what is happening, to recognize that it is happening to lots of people, that the pattern of events is similar, that the emotions experienced are commonly shared, and that the whole process is not inevitable – you *can* bring about change.

SELF-ASSESSMENT EXERCISES AND SCENARIOS

Self-assessment exercises are included at various points throughout the book so you can assess how relevant the general arguments being made are to you. They are designed to encourage you to reflect upon your experiences of violence or aggression and your feelings about them. If completed sequentially, they build up to give you a reasonably comprehensive picture of your involvement in, reactions to, and understanding of, aggressive or violent incidents. They can be used to monitor changes too: self-assessment can be repeated after an interval of perhaps a year or so or after a particularly significant incident. If you retain the originals for comparison purposes, you will be able to identify areas of change. If changes are occurring, whether positive or negative, you can try to pinpoint the likely reasons so as to improve your chances of controlling the nature of future changes.

I have also used hypothetical scenarios to illustrate some of the principles outlined in the text. Normally, these ask you to say what you would do in the situation outlined and then guidelines are offered about the alternative courses of action available. Again, it is possible to use these scenarios to monitor changes in your perspective over time. Both the self-assessment exercises and the scenarios are designed primarily to be used by the individual reader. They can, however, be used by groups in, for example, training workshops.

The first exercise starts the process of self-assessment by looking at your own experiences of aggression and violence. The purpose of this is to get you to focus on the patterns of aggression and violence which you have encountered across your lifetime. Your description of your experiences can be as detailed or as sketchy as you like; the value of the exercise lies in getting you to think about the characteristics of the people and of the situations which have been associated with violence. The exercise encourages self-reflection: how did you react? Has your style of reaction changed as you have grown older? Take some time over this exercise, write down your memories and keep the notes to refer back to later as you work through this book.

SELF-ASSESSMENT EXERCISE 1:
YOUR OWN EXPERIENCE OF AGGRESSION AND VIOLENCE

While accepting that violence and aggression happen to other people, many individuals will deny that they are present in their own lives. The purpose of this exercise is for you to examine your own life to check whether violence and aggression are part of your experience. For the moment, focus only upon incidents where **you** have been the victim.

Break your life into four periods: your childhood, your adolescence, your adulthood until six months ago, and now.

For each period list:

1. the types of violence or aggression you experienced;
2. the sort of people who acted as aggressors in each case;
3. the context in which the events occurred (for example, work or leisure);
4. how you reacted during and after the attack;
5. how frequently each sort of incident occurred.

There are no statistics against which you can compare your own experience of violence or aggression. The value of doing the exercise lies not in establishing how typical your experience is, but in establishing the backdrop for appreciating how your experiences of aggression or violence now relate to your earlier experiences, particularly those not associated with your working life. It will bring to the surface recollections of unpleasant events which may colour how you deal with aggression or violence now, and allows you to explore how your reactions to aggression have changed as you have matured.
　　You might specifically consider the following questions:

● If you have an extensive history of having to deal with aggression, do you believe that you have become the 'perpetual victim', or have you worked up strategies to deflect and control attacks?

● If you have very little experience of violence, do you feel immune from it or do you feel anxious that you would not know what to do if attacked?

The answers to these questions will differ between people. The important thing is to know the answer which *you* would give, whatever it might happen to be.

Chapter Two

Explaining Aggression

DISTINGUISHING BETWEEN ASSERTIVENESS, AGGRESSION AND VIOLENCE

When trying to explain aggression, it is useful to start by highlighting the differences between aggression, violence and assertiveness. In everyday conversation, the distinctions between these are often blurred and this can be a disadvantage when deciding how to deal with these three different types of behaviour. What they all share is that they involve confrontation. Where they differ is in the form of, and the motivation for, this confrontation.

Assertiveness is insisting on your rights or opinions. It involves claiming recognition from others that, within the constraints of the law, you have the right to decide how you think, feel and act.

Aggression is typically defined by psychologists as any form of behaviour intended to harm or injure someone against his or her wishes. This means that intentionally harming someone else is not aggression if the injured party wished this to happen. For instance, if during sexual intercourse a partner wants to be slapped or handled roughly, the act would not be considered aggressive because it was invited. Aggression entails any form of injury, including psychological or emotional injuries. So, for instance, shaming, frightening or threatening someone all constitute aggression.

Violence is defined as acts in which there is a deliberate attempt to inflict physical harm. Accidental harm does not comprise violence. This distinction between intended and accidental harm is made both in our everyday lives and in the legal system.

The distinction between assertiveness and aggression is worth emphasizing in the context of the activities of the caring professions.

Being able to be assertive is important for many of the people with whom members of the caring professions work. It is the means whereby individuality and identity are constructed and maintained, often in situations where both are attacked. Institutionalization, the gradual disintegration of individuality as the person conforms more and more to the requirements of the regime of an institution such as a hospital or hostel, has been described in many of the settings in which carers work. It has advantages for the institution in that it makes management of the patient or resident easier, but there are costs too. Independence and self-reliance decay and the chances of recovery or rehabilitation are eroded. Assertiveness can be used by the client as an antidote to counteract the effects of institutionalization.

Assertiveness is not only important within institutions, it is useful for clients in the community. Much social work and counselling would be unnecessary if clients were capable of being assertive in the pursuit of their own rights in such areas as employment, housing or welfare benefits. In fact, many teachers see the propagation of assertiveness as a major task for education. However, while assertiveness in principle may be valued, there is often a problem in practice. This is because assertiveness can slip into aggression. Often people do not know how to claim their own rights except through attacking the rights of others. In other cases, when assertiveness fails to achieve the desired recognition of their rights, people become aggressive. Carers often believe that they must tolerate aggression from clients in order to allow them the opportunity to develop more sophisticated ways of expressing themselves. You might find it useful to consider what forms of aggression you are willing to tolerate from different categories of people. Self-assessment Exercise 2 will help you to do this.

Being successfully assertive without being aggressive takes great skill, and it is a skill which all carers should try to acquire. Carers need to be assertive on their own behalf with their clients, patients, or pupils but they also need to be assertive with other people and with institutions on behalf of those for whom they care.

PSYCHOLOGICAL EXPLANATIONS OF AGGRESSION

In explaining aggression and violence psychologists have usually distinguished between *instrumental* and *emotional* forms of aggres-

SELF-ASSESSMENT EXERCISE 2:
TOLERABLE AGGRESSION AND VIOLENCE

Basically, this exercise allows you to examine where you draw the line between what is acceptable behaviour and what is not, and how this is modified by characteristics of the culprit. The assessment also allows you to consider how your perspective has changed since you started your career and how it compares with the attitudes and expectations that you believe other people in the profession have.

Following is a list of various types of aggression or violence, exhibited by different types of people in different sorts of situation. As the list is meant to cover the sorts of incidents which occur across a number of caring professions, some may be irrelevant to your work so just ignore those. In the first column, tick those behaviours which you would currently tolerate as an acceptable part of your job and which you would not report to your manager or senior colleague. This is not an easy task, because in each case it is possible to argue that you cannot say what you would do in the abstract; the precise circumstances would determine your response. However, respond to the checklist in a way which reflects how you think you would be most likely to react or have found that you typically react. In the second column, tick all those behaviours which you would have accepted when you first started to practise. In the third column, tick all those which you think that other members of your profession would typically tolerate.

	What you would tolerate now	What you used to tolerate	What others would tolerate

Where the aggressor is a child:
Swearing/cursing
Threats of violence
Pushing/shoving
Scratching
Punching
Kicking
Attack with weapon

continued

continued _____

	What you would tolerate now	What you used to tolerate	What others would tolerate
Where the aggressor is an adult:			
Swearing/cursing			
Threats of violence			
Pushing/shoving			
Scratching			
Punching			
Kicking			
Attack with weapon			
Where the aggressor is elderly:			
Swearing/cursing			
Threats of violence			
Pushing/shoving			
Scratching			
Punching			
Kicking			
Attack with weapon			
Where the aggressor has diminished responsibility (e.g. emotionally distraught; in extreme pain; dementing, etc.):			
Swearing/cursing			
Threats of violence			
Pushing/shoving			
Scratching			
Punching			
Kicking			
Attack with weapon			
Where a group of aggressors is involved:			
Swearing/Cursing			
Threats of violence			
Pushing/shoving			
Scratching			
Punching			
Kicking			
Attack with weapon			

Having done this exercise, it is useful to compare any differences in your levels of tolerance across types of aggressor which become apparent. It is useful to examine whether your personal norms of tolerance have changed and over what period. It is also useful to see how far you consider yourself similar in the norms you apply to other members of your profession. It may be even more valuable to see whether your perception of the norms others operate is accurate, by asking colleagues to complete the self-assessment exercise independently.

sion or violence. Instrumental aggression or violence is primarily a means towards some other end. The psychiatrist who is stabbed whilst a client attempts to steal some psychotropic drug is hurt so that the client might escape, not because the client is angry or upset with the psychiatrist. In contrast, emotional, or, as it is sometimes called, angry violence, deliberately inflicts injury. In this case, doing damage is an end in itself, and any instrumental value it has exists purely at a psychological level. A nurse who is attacked when he or she refuses to administer additional medication is not attacked in order to convince him or her that such medication should be provided; the attack is driven by anger rather than by any rational expectation that the nurse will be persuaded to hand over the drug. Most psychological attempts to explain aggression and violence have focused on the emotional variety. Instrumental violence is thought to be sufficiently explained by fact of its being instrumental.

There are three main types of psychological explanation for the occurrence of aggression and violence: the instinct explanation, the social or cultural learning explanation and the aversive stimulation explanation. These three theories will be described briefly in turn.

THE INSTINCT EXPLANATION

This assumes that aggression is a need like the need to sleep and the need to eat. It is not learned, it is biologically determined and inevitable. If aggression is suppressed, the desire for it builds up and it will break out eventually. According to this view, we are all aggressive, we are all violent; we differ only in the ways and situations in which we allow our aggression to be released. Most notably we are supposed to differ in the extent to which we can direct our aggressive impulses into activities which are socially accepted, for example, into sporting rivalries or economic competition or national defence. Psychoanalytic explanations of aggression (for instance, Freudian theories) fall broadly into this category (Moore, 1995).

Within this framework, the aggressive instinct is assumed to have developed because it has survival value for the species as a whole (self-protection and sustenance rely in large part upon competition and aggression) and, to a lesser extent, for individual members of it. However, such an explanation of aggression has little practical value because it has little predictive power – it cannot say when aggression will occur, what form it will take, or what interventions are likely to control it. It is even impossible to give a partially realistic example of an aggressive incident which might be exclusively explained by recourse to the instinct model. As soon as we consider actual incidents, it becomes evident that other types of explanation must also be taken into account.

THE SOCIAL OR CULTURE LEARNING EXPLANATION

According to this view, aggression is not inevitable; aggression and violence are behaviours like all others and are learned (Durkin, 1995). Two types of learning are said to be involved: *instrumental* and *observational*.

INSTRUMENTAL LEARNING

Instrumental learning is said to occur when a behaviour is reinforced through rewards, therefore making it more likely to recur in the future. This does not only apply to good behaviour – aggressive acts which are rewarded will also be produced more frequently. Rewards can be material (for example, financial), social (for example, the awarding of status), or psychological (for example, by generating emotional satisfaction). There are many examples of violent incidents where instrumental learning may explain what has happened. Take the case of the child whose parents praise her for 'standing up for herself' when pushed around by other children; they commend her when she hits out when she is faced with any offence or insult. The child will be more likely to exhibit violence in that type of situation subsequently and moreover, if she continues to be praised for such violence, the violent response is likely to generalize. For instance, she might strike out at a nurse who hurts her in the course of administering an injection or other treatment. The child sees violence as the appropriate response to *any* harm done to her, whether intended or not. Such generalization of learned responses is limited usually by a process of *differential reinforcement*. For instance, parents who see the child lash out at a nurse are likely to scold or reprimand, thus indicating one of the boundaries of appropriate violent self-defence.

Behaviours which result in the removal of something which is regarded as unpleasant are also reinforced and are likely to recur or become more frequent. For instance, a patient who prevents another patient bullying by retaliating physically is likely to be encouraged to use violence as a coping strategy in the future because the violence had proven capable of ending something which was unpleasant (the bullying).

OBSERVATIONAL LEARNING

Many other aggressive behaviours are believed to be learned through observing others. This observational learning is sometimes called *social modelling*. Bandura (1969) and his colleagues found some evidence that children who watched someone behaving in a violent way would, when subsequently given the opportunity, behave in a similar manner. There are many studies with adults which show the results of modelling too. While children may learn *how* to be aggressive while watching others, adults appear to learn *when* it is appropriate to be aggressive by watching others. Adults are normally very aware of the social expectations concerning the appropriateness of violence but their appreciation of these expectations can be changed by watching other people in their situation. For instance, in a crowded hospital emergency waiting room, the arrival of one patient who starts to abuse staff because he or she is being made to wait can trigger impatience, irascibility and direct abuse from others who are also waiting (especially those who have been waiting longer). The expectation of patient compliance and, indeed, patience, is breached; the action of the newcomer acts as a learning experience. Observational learning can explain how a violent mood or ethos can spread through a group of unrelated people who just happen to be in the same situation at the same time.

ADVANTAGES OF THE SOCIAL/CULTURE LEARNING EXPLANATION

One of the advantages of the learning explanation for aggression and violence is that it can explain the existence of cultural and subcultural differences in the amount and form of violence exhibited. Anthropological evidence indicates that some societies emphasize the value of pacifism and measure achievement in terms of personal gratification rather than in terms of dominance or power over others. Similarly, sociological evidence proves that subcultures differ greatly in the ways in which they will allow aggression to be expressed. In some, aggression is expected to be expressed physically; in others, verbally. Subcultures also differ in who they expect to be aggressive, to whom and when. For instance, there are big differences between the ways in which men and women are expected to express their aggression. Because people learn from their cultures and subcultures what behaviours are appropriate, the forms of violence and aggression members of each subculture choose to use, when they choose to use them and against whom they are used are dictated by norms established within their societies.

This type of explanation of aggression has value for practitioners in the caring professions because it suggests that if you know the norms which control the form, frequency and targets of aggression in the subculture in which you work, you should be better able to predict incidents. It means that the behaviour of individual clients or patients can be analysed in relation to their social background. Of course, this is more possible in some practice contexts than in others and it assumes that you already know something about the individual's background – there are many situations where a practitioner must intervene without having had the opportunity to acquire relevant background information. So, for instance, the social or cultural learning approach to aggression might be particularly useful for a teacher who can learn the norms about aggressive behaviour which operate in his or her school and thus predict confrontations. However, for the purposes of prediction, the socio-cultural learning approach is most useful if allied to an analysis of the social roles attributed to participants in the action. For example, in a school the norm might be that boys in Class 4X are unruly with young female teachers but that one, Gavin, has the role of the class ruffian and it is his task to initiate the confrontations with teachers. Knowing both the norm and the role of Gavin is important in the process of predicting incidents and developing strategies for coping with them.

LIMITATIONS OF THE SOCIAL/CULTURE LEARNING EXPLANATION

While the social learning approach, especially if linked to role analysis, is useful, it does have limitations. It tends to underestimate the significance of the active and constructive role of the learner in interpreting both the nature of the reward–punishment regime and the relevance of the experience of any model. Current theories of learning emphasize that the learner attributes meaning to experiences on the basis of a frame of reference which is acquired over years and which is capable of transforming the meaning of events. For example, I may recognize that I am being rewarded by my friends for acting in a cruel way to some stranger but I may discount their praise and avoid further cruelty because I know that such behaviour is wrong. What is wrong or right I know from my entire history of learning experiences. This can mean that immediate learning experiences do not result in obvious and interpretable changes in behaviour or knowledge; there are many cases of clients who do not change their behaviour patterns even though they are seriously punished for maintaining them. This limitation of the social learning approach is overcome to a great extent when it is integrated into a situational analysis and this is described later in this chapter.

THE AVERSIVE STIMULATION EXPLANATION

Unpleasant or aversive stimulation increases a person's level of physiological arousal (their blood pressure, heart rate, adrenaline flow, etc.). It is thought that people are biologically pre-programmed to attempt to avoid such heightened arousal, which is experienced as abnormal and unacceptable. Aggression is seen as only one of a range of responses designed to bring about a reduction in arousal levels, largely by eradicating the source of the unpleasant stimulation.

This explanation predicts that aggression may be the preferred response to aversive stimulation under certain circumstances: if other types of response (for example, avoidance or flight) are impossible; if there are cues in the situation which are associated with aggression (for example, the presence of a gun or, in some cultures, particular types of music, clothes, pictures, even smells); if the individual has found aggression a rewarding and successful solution in the past.

FRUSTRATION–AGGRESSION HYPOTHESIS

The frustration–aggression hypothesis is a special example of the aversive stimulation explanation. The frustration–aggression hypothesis proposed originally in 1939 by Dollard, Doob, Miller, Mowrer and Sears was very simple: all aggression was supposed to be preceded by frustration of some sort. Frustration occurs, according to this hypothesis, when a person cannot, for whatever reason, achieve set goals. There is considerable evidence that frustration can cause aggression, especially if it is intense or if aggression is seen to be likely, even indirectly, to be a means towards goal attainment. However, frustration does not always result in aggression. For instance, where it does not result in anger, or where it is seen to have a justifiable origin, frustration is unlikely to initiate aggression (Berkowitz, 1969; 1994).

PAINFUL EXPERIENCES AND AGGRESSION

Frustration is only one sort of unpleasant feeling that people wish to avoid. Physical pain is obviously another. But noise, crowding and heat can affect people in exactly the same way. Just as frustration can find alternative expression, so other unpleasant experiences do not necessarily give rise to aggression. Whether they do or not depends on the precise nature of the situation in which they occur, the past history of the person involved and his or her genetic predispositions. Painful experiences can result in avoidance or flight instead of aggression. There is considerable empirical evidence to suggest that painful experiences are most likely to result in aggression if the individual has a history of aggressive responses (particularly if these have been found to be effective in gaining rewards), if aggression is likely to eradicate them, or if cues for violence are prevalent in the situation.

If much of aggression and violence can be considered simply as a predictable response to an unpleasant experience, the frequency with which practitioners experience hostility becomes hardly surprising. Most of them are, after all, called in precisely at those times when their clients or patients are dealing with events which are unpleasant and distressing. The nurse in an emergency room of a hospital will be habitually dealing with people who are in pain and frightened. Sometimes the practitioner will be the source of frustration and fear. The social worker who tells a woman that her husband must be compulsorily detained in a psychiatric hospital, or the health visitor who suggests that a child is deaf, or the doctor who explains that a condition is inoperable, all create the emotional potential for aggression.

AN INTERACTIONIST SITUATIONAL APPROACH

While each of the three psychological explanations of aggression and violence just outlined have some merit, they are all somewhat uni-dimensional and inadequate to model the complexities of real violent situations. Real violence takes place against a background of many interacting factors: the social norms of the situation, the social history of the individual, and, not least, the social meanings embedded in the specific situation. The situational approach would argue that most acts of violence are the result of a wide range of interacting factors linked with each other and tied to the people involved, the contexts in which these people interact, and the specific type of interaction between these people which immediately precedes a violent act. This type of explanation for aggression is essentially based in the theories of social psychology.

An actual example of violence against a psychiatrist might help to illustrate the complexity. A 21- year-old woman hit her psychiatrist across the head and repeatedly punched him about the torso when he suggested that she might consider having an abortion. As she did so, she shouted 'You should know I'm a Catholic'. No simple explanation of this young woman's violence in terms of outraged religious sentiment will work when one considers the case a little further. The woman had been required to see this psychiatrist after she had been picked up by the police walking in the middle of a busy road against the traffic. This was the second occasion on which this had happened; the night before she had been taken to the local psychiatric hospital by the police after walking in the middle of the road but had been discharged 30 minutes later after being diagnosed as suffering from stress rather than a mental illness. This was despite the fact that she had for several years been regarded as possible personality-disordered and had been in psychiatric wards where she had witnessed assaults on staff. At the time that he saw her, the psychiatrist knew that she had three children, all of whom had been taken into care. Each of her children had been fathered by a different man, and what the psychiatrist did not know was that one of these men (whom the woman now hated) had just gained a residence order for his child, claiming the woman was an incapable mother. The woman explained to the psychiatrist that she was facing eviction from her house by the local council because she had been found throwing stones at her next-door-neighbour's children. The night before she had been picked up by the police, she had been deserted by the man with whose child she was pregnant.

Many factors in this woman's past history, current life circumstances, psychiatric condition and immediate situation can be seen to be likely to play a part in precipitating her violence. Any of the three major psychological theoretical explanations of aggression would be inadequate alone to account for her behaviour. Even taken together, they offer only a broad interpretative framework. In fact, any comprehensive explanation of most violent incidents will involve many interacting factors. This is why an interactionist situational approach is needed; it draws upon social psychological theories which account for the ways societal structures and psychological processes interact to determine action.

Factors associated with the people involved will include their age, education, criminal histories, attitudes, socio-economic status, race, mental health, sex and life stress. The context of the interaction will differ in terms of its location, the time of day at which it occurs, the number of people present and the relationships between them and, not least, the geographical or architectural structure of the space in which the interaction occurs. There is no one integrative theoretical framework which currently exists that can be used to explain how all of these factors interact in generating a particular piece of violence at a specific place at a single moment in time. A whole variety of different social psychological theories are used, each relevant for a different aspect of the violent event.

The advantage for the practitioner of the situational approach lies not so much in its power to explain, but in its power to direct analysis. It indicates the variety of factors which must be monitored in order to understand how violence operates in practice.

INTERPRETING SITUATIONS

Our responses to aversive stimuli are greatly influenced by the way we perceive the situation. People will tolerate considerable pain and discomfort or frustration without becoming aggressive if they interpret the situation as having arisen unintentionally or accidentally. It is, of course, important to add that there are situations in which people will be aggressive even though they know that the discomfort was not deliberately intended. The inhibitors which would normally curtail aggression in response to unintended hurt can break down; for example, the ability to inhibit the expression of aggression is markedly affected by the intake of alcohol and certain drugs. There is a body of evidence to support the popular idea that alcohol in moderate quantities will increase aggressive behaviour, though it should be said that there are big differences between individuals in how disinhibited they are by alcohol. Individual inhibitions against violence can also be eroded if the person is enmeshed in a group activity: personal responsibility for decisions is subdued and disinhibition occurs.

The particular value of the aversive stimuli explanation of aggression and violence lies in its power to bridge the gap between the instinct and social learning theories. It acknowledges the biological and physiological foundations for aggression but also emphasizes the way socially determined ways of interpreting events will channel the potential for aggression and its expression. It shows that behaviour is not predetermined by instincts nor moulded solely on the basis of learning or modelling. Instead, it recognizes that there is a complex symbolic world through which people navigate a course and in which aggression has an important role. The meaning of, and reasons for, an aversive event will in part determine whether it elicits violence or aggression. But the potential aggressive response will also have alternative meanings (instrumental and symbolic) which will influence whether it actually occurs. The individual's understanding of the event has a big part to play in directing aggression. The perception of the cause for the aversive experience, the mitigating circumstances which may apply, the impact of aggression upon the impression about oneself to be created in the minds of others, the likely benefits of aggression; all these have a part to play in predicting aggression. In acknowledging these factors, the aversive stimuli explanation is acknowledging the importance of the way people gather, store and handle information about violence and aggression. It is also implicitly arguing for the malleability of aggression since these habits of thought can be influenced and changed.

Given the role of most of the caring professions it may be impossible to remove the aversive stimuli which encourage aggression. It is therefore more practical for practitioners to modify the way in which these stimuli are interpreted or the ways in which the aggression is expressed.

To return to an earlier example: the nurse in the example on p.13 may not be able to remove the fear, pain or much of the anxiety but she might be able to ensure that when further medication is not immediately available the delay is explained so that it does not become another cause for distress and she is not seen as being deliberately hostile.

For the practitioner, the aversive stimuli explanation of aggression and violence also has some value because it highlights the type of circumstances in which they are likely to occur. This type of explanation does make it possible to anticipate the broad range of situations in which violence is likely and the sort of factors which will increase its likelihood.

INSTRUMENTAL VIOLENCE

Explanations for aggression tend to focus upon the 'emotional' forms, where harm is deliberate but not caused with some ulterior motive in mind. Instrumental violence is considered to be a means to an end and tends to be treated as goal-directed behaviour, requiring no other explanation. This is unsatisfactory. In practice, an act of aggression will often have both emotional and instrumental facets. Take, for instance, the recently reported case of a head teacher who was threatened and then had her school fire-bombed by youths whom she had reported to the police for breaking into the car of another teacher. The attack was premeditated and designed to terrorize the head teacher. It can consequently be said to be instrumental: it had a clear purpose. Yet it was also motivated by anger and hatred. The desire for vengeance has a strong emotional component. Explanations for such aggression must encompass both an analysis of the instrumental benefits of the act and its emotional undertone.

It might be added that conversely something which is labelled predominantly emotional violence may well have an instrumental undertone. For instance, sexual or racial harassment, which are both forms of aggression, may appear to be driven by emotional reactions at one level, but there is an important sense in which they are also motivated by the struggle for relative power between individuals and between social groups.

Many of the violent incidents which involve practitioners entail this sort of mixture of emotional and instrumental aggression. Knowing about the triggers and risk factors described in Chapter 3 is useful when seeking to anticipate violence but it is also valuable to analyse whether there is any reason to believe that violence against you might achieve some ulterior purpose. If it might, even if only in the eyes of the potential attacker, then the risk is heightened. Of course, goals which are pursued with violence may not be rational. There need be no logical relationship between the violence and the expected outcome – the connection may exist only in the mind of the attacker. Consequently, it is enormously difficult to anticipate when someone will see violence as a rational course of action designed to achieve realistic goals. However, the practitioner who builds into an assessment of risk an examination of the instrumental payoffs of any aggression improves the likelihood of being able to take sensible precautions against an attack.

VIOLENCE IN A GROUP CONTEXT

So far in discussing the forms of aggression and violence it has been implicit that these are the acts of individuals. In fact, it is necessary to draw a distinction between individuals who are aggressive or violent, and groups or organizations which are aggressive or violent. Violence can emanate from all sorts of groups: from those as informal and unstructured as crowds to those as complex and hierarchical as large corporations. It can range from the police-stoning street riot to the corporate vandalism involved in making entire communities redundant. Similarly, groups can engage in aggression: street gangs

can induce terror with threats, business consortia can foster despera-
tion with rumours of closure.

Obviously, even in groups or organizations it is individuals who
do the violence or make the aggression manifest but the underlying
pattern of responsibility is different. The decision to be aggressive or
violent does not rest entirely with the individual. Responsibility is
diffused across group or organization members, and such diffusion
has long been assumed to partially explain why people as members
of groups will be more violent, and more irrational and full of hostile
emotions than they will when acting as individuals (Prentice-Dunn,
1990). They feel anonymous in the group and that they can get away
metaphorically, and sometimes literally, with murder because they
are an unidentifiable part of the mass (McPhail, 1994). This process of
losing the self in the group is known as *de-individuation*.

There is a contradictory argument which has been generated to
explain why people behave more violently when part of a crowd.
This suggests that extremes of behaviour occur in groups not because people lose their sense of self or forget the norms which usually control their behaviour, but rather because new norms emerge
within a crowd in a specific situation (Staub, 1991). So, for instance,
in a street riot, the crowd can generate the idea that it is necessary to
protect itself from the police; stoning the police becomes the norm for
the situation, even though it abrogates commonly-held pre-existing
norms.

More importantly, even well-organized groups, when in high
stress situations, tend to become concerned with maintaining group
cohesiveness and survival to the exclusion of rationality. Under such
circumstances, they become subject to what Janis (1976) called
'groupthink'. This is a state characterized by the belief that whatever
the group decides is right and morally acceptable and any challenge
to the group's decision by a group member constitutes treachery.
Violence towards anyone not allied to the group is then regarded as
morally appropriate.

It is evident that forms of violence and aggression involving
groups or organizations must be treated differently from those concerning isolated individuals. While it is probably true that the caring
professions mainly face violence from individuals, it is also true that
family groups can be a considerable threat for those practitioners
working in the community, and groupings amongst youths can generate incidents in educational and residential settings (Scheidlinger,
1994).

It has become clear in considering the explanations of violence and aggression that neither can be explained in terms of individual psychological processes. Violence and aggression must be seen as embedded in the interactions between two or more people, in the particular circumstances in which they find themselves and against the backdrop of the cultural norms which guide their actions. It is for this reason that social psychological theories are most useful for practitioners seeking to predict, and then cope with, aggression.

CHAPTER SUMMARY

❏ Aggression, assertiveness and violence should be differentiated. Aggression is any behaviour intended to harm somebody against their wishes. Assertiveness is claiming recognition from others of your right to decide how you think, feel and act, within the constraints of the law. Violence is any deliberate attempt to inflict physical harm.

❏ In explaining aggression and violence, psychologists distinguish between emotional and instrumental forms. The instrumental variety can be explained in terms of motivation to achieve a particular goal. For emotional aggression or violence there are three main psychological explanations: the instinct explanation, the social or cultural learning explanation; and the aversive stimulation explanation. The clear distinction between instrumental and emotional aggression is probably not viable in practice since in most cases instrumental aggression usually will have a substantial emotional component.

❏ The instinct explanation assumes aggression is a biologically determined need.

❏ The social or cultural learning explanation assumes that we learn how and when and to whom to be aggressive by normal processes of learning (that is, responding to reward–punishment regimes). It asserts that we can also learn aggression vicariously, through merely observing others being rewarded or punished for their aggressive actions.

❏ The aversive stimulation explanation suggests that aggression occurs when some unpleasant stimulus increases physiological arousal. Aggression is only one of the possible ways by which such arousal may be reduced. Aggression will be the outcome of aversive stimulation only under certain circumstances, for example, if other responses are impossible or if aggression is likely to be rewarded or if there are strong cues for violence in the situation.

❏ The interactionist situation approach to explaining and predicting aggression argues that real violence is determined by many interacting factors, such as the history of the individual and the norms of the situation.

❏ How people respond in a situation which may stimulate violence or aggression is dependent in large part upon their interpretation of the social and personal meaning of the situation.

❏ Violence in the context of groups of people needs to be explained in different ways. Processes of groupthink, diffusion of responsibility and de-individuation enhance the potential for violence in the group context.

❏ Practitioners wishing to use psychological explanations for aggression in order to develop better methods for coping with aggression and violence may be best advised to adopt a social psychological approach. This focuses on the interaction of individual determinants with interpersonal and intergroup factors in the context of wider social norms and proscriptions.

Chapter Three

Predicting Aggression

ASSESSING THE RISK OF ATTACK

General theories of aggression clearly have to be distinguished from the specific explanations for particular violent incidents which are commonly produced by the participants or by observers. Accounts by observers are likely to emphasize the personality of the perpetrator and the unique combination of traits which characterize him or her. Accounts by the perpetrator are likely to focus upon the context and the unique combination of circumstances which came together in the situation. Everyone evidences biases when explaining events (Kahneman, Slovic and Tversky, 1982) and there are three prime biases:

- **actor–observer bias:** when asked to explain their own behaviour, people do so in terms of the situation or context that constrains and determines their actions. When they explain the behaviour of others, they do so in terms of the personal characteristics of those individuals (for example, their intelligence, impulsivity or social skills).
- **typicality bias:** people believe that their own motives, beliefs and attitudes are typical of everyone else. They find it difficult to conceive that other people are motivated by different considerations or hold quite different views.
- **desirability bias:** people explain their own desirable or acceptable behaviour in terms of their own personal qualities. They explain their undesirable behaviour in terms of factors that they cannot control (for example, chance or accidental occurrences). This is clearly one way of discounting responsibility for any actions that are subsequently reviled.

Commonsense explanations of events are riddled with the effects of such biases. Biases of this sort make it difficult to use personal experience to derive generalizations about the risks of violence in specific situations from particular people. The interpretation of the evidence which might allow you to draw such conclusions is distorted by these powerful cognitive biases. In contrast, socio-psychological theories are concerned with generic principles rather than the idiosyncrasies of specific cases. They provide insights about the likelihood of violence at a very general level and suggest a list of clues which are indicators of the risk involved.

The bulk of evidence from empirical studies (Webster *et al.*, 1994) indicates that generally the risk of violence is greater if:

• the person is a member of a group or subculture where physical violence is the norm. If violent, the person therefore will experience no loss of face and may, in fact, benefit;
• the person has a history of violence – violence is then assumed to be a preferred strategy for dealing with problems;
• the person is aroused by some aversive stimuli (especially if these are interpreted to be deliberate attempts to hurt and are directed especially at the person concerned);
• the person is disinhibited (through drugs, alcohol, de-individuation, physical illnesses such as brain damage, and so on);
• the person expects the violence to be rewarded either materially or through social approval;
• the person believes no other action is possible. This may be associated with a belief that the person is not in control of his or her own actions. This owes something to the instinct theories of aggression.

There are, however, other clues which can be used when calculating risk in a specific situation which are not dependent on the explanations of aggression. These stem from empirical research on the expression of aggression. Risk is greater in a specific situation if:

• the person has been threatening violence – threats can have an end in themselves if they are designed to control or scare but they also represent a statement of intention and intentions are the best predictors of action known – much better than attitudes, beliefs or values;
• there are cues to violence in the situation, such as the presence of knives, choppers, or other weapons; someone else already acting violently;
• the person manifests the physiological signs of high arousal. The problem with this is that these are by no means simple to predict;

some people display a flushed skin reflecting raised blood pressure, perspiration, increased muscle tension, heightened respiration rate and pulse, and even nausea but for others arousal results in the loss of colour and great stillness. The real clue to look for seems to be any shift from the individual's typical state.

● the person is verbally abusive – verbal abuse is a frequent but not inevitable precursor to violence. Also, tone, pitch and speed of talk can change. Again it is variation from the pattern which is typical of the person which should be treated with caution;

● there is peer group pressure being exerted upon the person to be violent;

● the person is showing non-verbal signs of imminent violence: invasion of personal space (that invisible bubble which surrounds each of us and which we regard as our inalienable mobile territory); maintenance of eye contact for prolonged periods so that it becomes uncomfortable; rapid unpredictable arm movements especially involving pointing; clenching and unclenching teeth or fists; etc. Again, non-verbal signs can only be interpreted against the backdrop of the person's typical behaviour. Deviations from the norm are what become useful cues.

Taken together, these clues can provide a useful basis for calculations of risk. But the practitioner using the list as a guide must understand that there are no cast iron rules for predicting specific occurrences of violence. There is no set equation which summarizes which constellation of clues will always precede violence. Each violent incident is unique. In some, none of these clues will be present. But in the majority, at least some of them will be there to provide a warning for those who can see them.

TRIGGER FACTORS

The situational analysis of violent incidents has led psychologists to suggest that there are trigger factors which can change an interaction between a practitioner and a patient from being potentially violent to being *actually* violent. These 'trigger factors' largely parallel the risk factors just outlined, though one or two are peculiar to the practitioner – client relationship.

The most common trigger factors are:

1.   An intensification of the aversive-stimulation, for example, exacerbation of the experience of pain by insisting that the patient

waits an inordinate length of time for treatment, or the imposi-
tion of statutory authority.

2. Onset of disinhibition created by the use of drugs, etc.
3. The sudden perceived absence of an alternative option to the
    use of violence.
4. The arrival in the situation of cues which reinforce violence, for
    example, images of violence such as photographs depicting
    martial arts, or the presence of other people, for instance, peer
    group members, who will be seen to approve of violence.
5. A perceived increase in the potential reward for violence.
6. The use of words or phrases known to be provocative to the
    person concerned (these are sometimes called barbs).
7. The experience of sudden major life changes or the advent of
    new stressors.
8. Attempts to interpret the individual's behaviour as psychotic
    when the individual regards his or her behaviour as normal.

VIOLENCE, ALCOHOL AND DRUGS

Commonsense links violence to both alcohol and drug use. The actual connection is quite complex and there is a vast literature on it
(Collins and Messerschmidt, 1993). In so far as alcohol or drugs act to
reduce self-control in frustrating situations, they have been shown to
be associated with violence. In the case of alcohol, moderate levels of
intoxication do not increase violence unless the individual is threatened or provoked and only then if no non-aggressive alternative is
possible (Gustafson, 1994). There is also evidence that women, even
when provoked while intoxicated, are less likely than men to react
with violence (Giancola and Zeichner, 1995). Intoxicated people are
less likely to curtail their aggression when faced with the possibility
of subsequent retaliation or punishment (Weisman and Taylor, 1994).

The drugs–violence nexus has been the subject of much debate.
Goldstein (1985) suggested that drug use and trafficking are both ae-
tiological factors in violence and he analysed three forms of linkage.
First, drugs can cause violence because they induce sychopharmaco-
logical changes in users which alter behaviour. Second, drugs can result in instrumental violence: in order to get drugs users will steal
and assault. Third, the drug market creates societal changes (for example, gangs, law enforcement regimes) which themselves precipitate violence. Most sociological researchers now argue that the major
reason for drug-related violence is economic (McBride and Scharter,
1990) and related to the drug-distribution system (Collins, 1990).

THE DANGEROUSNESS CHECKLIST

The *Dangerousness Checklist* summarizes the questions that you should ask yourself when trying to assess the risk inherent in a situation. It is a simple reminder of the practical import of the explanations and predictive cues for aggression discussed in Chapters 2 and 3. The *Checklist* can be used as a barometer of the risk of violence, the idea being that you mentally run through the *Checklist* regularly prior to contacts with clients, patients or other clientele. In order to answer some of the questions it is necessary to have considerable information on the person you will be contacting. This will only be available to individual practitioners if good systems of information transmission are set up (especially across agencies, for example, police to social services and from them to the education system) and if better records of contacts and incidents are kept.

It should be noted that predictions of dangerousness have been found to be affected by assessors' preconceptions. It is difficult to make an assessment of dangerousness simply on the facts given, as other cultural expectations interfere with the rational assessment of information. For instance, Coontz *et al.* (1994) found that staff in psychiatric emergency rooms were likely to underestimate the dangerousness of female patients. This they explained in terms of gender-role expectations held by the staff.

VIOLENCE TOWARDS OTHERS

The notion of using predictors of behaviour is commonly accepted in the caring professions. One of the most widely used, yet controversial, set of predictors concerns child abuse. Researchers (Gardner and Gray, 1982) have shown that those who abuse their children tend to have an identifiable profile: they tend to be isolated from their family and friends, they are involved in marital conflicts, they wanted a child of the opposite sex, they live in deprived social and economic conditions, they have unrealistic expectations of the child's behaviour and perceive the child to be deliberately wilful or naughty, and they have an over-idealistic image of what parenthood should be like. They also tend to have no way of handling conflict other than by becoming violent. It is also possible to profile the child who is abused since prematurity, mental retardation, physical handicaps, and perinatal complications are over-represented in the abused population. The important point to remember about predictors is that they result

SELF-ASSESSMENT EXERCISE 3:
THE DANGEROUSNESS CHECKLIST

When assessing the extent of the risk of violence in a situation you are about to enter, you should consider the following questions. The more often you answer 'Yes', the greater the risk of violence.

Yes   No

Is the person I am dealing with facing high levels of stress?

Is the person likely to be drunk or on drugs?

Does the person have a history of violence?

Does the person have a history of criminal convictions?

Does the person have a history of psychiatric illness?

Does the person suffer from a medical condition which may result in loss of self-control?

Has the person verbally abused me in the past?

Has the person threatened me with violence in the past?

Has the person attacked me in the past?

Does the person perceive me as a threat to his/her children?

Does the person think of me as a threat to his/her liberty?

Does the person have unrealistic expectations of what I can do for him/her?

Does the person perceive me as wilfully unhelpful?

Have I felt anxious for my safety with this person before?

Are other people present who will reward the person for violence?

_____ continued _____

continued _____

Facing the client or patient, other cues should be examined. Again, the more times you answer 'Yes' in a situation, the greater the danger:

Yes   No

Is the person showing signs of atypical excitement or passivity?

Are there weapons or similar cues to violence in the room?

Is the person showing signs of atypical high arousal?

Is there a breakdown in the normal pattern of nonverbal communication?

Is the person showing signs of rapid mood swings?

Is the person showing oversensitivity to suggestions or criticisms?

The implications of the risk are greater if you answer 'Yes' to several of the following questions:

Yes   No

Am I alone and without back-up?

Are colleagues unaware of my whereabouts?

Am I without any means of raising the alarm if attacked?

Am I likely to be trapped without an escape route if the person becomes violent?

Am I unaware of how I react in violent situations?

Am I unaware of the assault cycle?

Am I unaware of the cultural norms which are likely to control this person's exhibition of violence?

Have I never considered what I would do if attacked?

in over-inclusion of suspects. Not all who have this profile will be abusers. The predictors simply allow attention to be focused upon people most at risk of abusing. These individuals can then be more intensively monitored.

Predictors can be used to identify children who are likely to be repeatedly involved in serious crimes later in life (Farrington, 1987). Farrington's argument is that there is continuity between childhood trouble and adult criminal behaviour, so that frequent serious offenders tend to have had: harsh or erratic parental discipline; parents whose attitude was cruel, passive or neglectful; poor parental supervision during childhood; and parents who were themselves in conflict before the child was eight years old. Again, not everyone with this profile becomes a criminal. The predictors act to target a broad group of people and will include some who would never become criminals. People with this type of background who remain law-abiding are characterized by higher intelligence, greater shyness, anxiety, and apathy, and the tendency to be withdrawn or obsessional. They also tend to come from families with fewer children and where the parents did not separate or become involved in serious conflicts. Farrington suggests that any intervention designed to prevent the shift into criminality (such as training for parents or the provision of special educational tutoring in schools) should be over-inclusive in its catchment. This approach means that the predictors can still be used even though they are somewhat insensitive to individual variations.

From the point of view of the practitioner seeking to avoid violent confrontation, both the predictors of child abuse and the predictors of frequent offending are tangentially useful because for a reasonably large number of practitioners (for example, social workers, probation officers, police officers), people with this background will comprise major client groups. It is therefore useful ancillary information in predicting behaviour.

BIASES AFFECTING CALCULATION OF RISK

The problem with relying upon estimates of risk is that people are notoriously bad at calculating probabilities accurately. People find it difficult to say whether an event has for instance a one in 10 or one in 100 chance of happening. Even when they are completely aware of all the necessary information, they tend to produce biased estimates. They are influenced by their own prejudices, by recent experiences, by their own emotional involvement, and so on. Estimates of risk are, therefore, rarely accurate. Becoming aware of the processes which influence your own probability calculations can be the first step towards more accurate perception of the risks entailed in any particular situation. There are three major biases which have been identified (Kahneman *et al.*, 1982): *availability, anchoring and adjustments,* and *representativeness,* and we will now look at these.

AVAILABILITY

People make poor estimates of the *frequency* of events. They tend to be overly influenced by the ease with which specific instances can be brought to mind. For instance, they may assess the risk of heart attacks among middle-aged men on the basis of the occurrence of such events among their own acquaintances because these are prominent in their memory. Obviously this leads to biased estimates of risk unless the number of instances recalled is proportional to the actual incidence rate. In fact, most estimates of risk are biased in this way because where examples are easily retrieved from memory, that class of event is deemed more frequent. So, someone who had a colleague who was physically assaulted would be likely to be influenced by the recollection of this event and assume that the frequency of assault was greater than it actually is. In such a case, estimates of risk are affected by familiarity with an example.

We are also influenced by the *importance* and *relevance* of the example. Both of these features will affect the ease with which it is initially stored in memory and subsequently retrieved. It is notable that, once alerted to a risk through personal experience, people can become selectively attentive to information relevant to it. For instance, the death of a good friend from a heart attack will result in the person paying more attention to reports of other such deaths. If the friend also smoked heavily, the link between smoking and coronary disease would be emphasized. Once established, this link would encourage the person to look for evidence of heavy smoking in all coronary cases. This can mean that a sort of snowball effect occurs with more and more examples which support the initial conclusion being stored away and used as the foundation for future calculations of risk. Of course, this has the effect of increasing the level of risk perceived.

The availability of examples is also affected by the *information retrieval strategy* adopted in the first place. Memories can be searched in myriad ways in order to generate relevant information for the calculation of probabilities. If the object is to estimate the probability of violence, the search could be organized around personal incidents recalled, press coverage of serious attacks recollected, conversations in which assaults were described, and so on. The method used for eliciting and organizing memories will bias the type and amount of information collected. For instance, self-relevant memories are more easily retrieved, especially if they provide a positive picture of the self. Probabilities based on such memories will be likely therefore to under-estimate the potential hazards. Basically, some retrieval strategies are more comprehensive and thus more effective than others in generating accurate estimates of probability.

Imagination also plays an important role in the evaluation of probabilities. The risk involved in an interchange with a client is evaluated by imagining contingencies with which it would be impossible to cope. If difficulties can be vividly imagined, the risk is likely to be judged higher. In contrast, when the imagination fails, risks are perceived to be less. This is all irrespective of the actual statistical probability of danger.

People are particularly influenced in estimates of risk by *preconceptions* about associations between events or things. If two things are believed to be associated with each other in popular belief, for example, red hair and fiery temper, when people are presented with one of the pair, they tend to assume the other is probably present regardless of whether they have any empirical justification for that assumption. For instance, if GPs in a particular area believe that a certain council estate is dangerous to visit at night, when they hear that a GP has been mugged at night somewhere in the area they are very likely to assume that it was on the council estate. They are also likely to remember the incident as occurring in the estate, even if later their assumption proves wrong. More importantly, this erroneous information will then feed into any further calculations of the risks of going to that estate.

ANCHORING AND ADJUSTMENT

In calculating risk, people tend to start from an initial estimate and then adjust this to produce a final estimate. They might assume that they have a one in 50 chance of being attacked in a year. This estimate will be modified to take account of additional information in particular situations. However, there is considerable evidence to show that people do not shift enough from their original estimate when faced with contradictory evidence. To extend the analogy: the anchor is not weighed. Instead it stays on the sea bed, immobile, and preventing appropriate movement in judgements of risk.

Bias due to anchoring is also exemplified in another way. People tend to extrapolate unjustifiably from one success to others. So, for instance, a practitioner who successfully handled a single potentially violent situation is likely to infer that the risks in other violent situations are lower than they actually are. It seems that people are more likely to assume that the same pattern of events will recur than they are to assume that there will be a break with what happened before.

REPRESENTATIVENESS

Many probability estimates require the person to say whether an event or an individual belongs to a particular category; if they do, assumptions can be made about the probability of them possessing certain characteristics. Typically, people fail to make use of the appropriate information when making such categorizations, ignoring the overall number of people or events in the category. If the description of the event or person fits the stereotype held of the category, the probability of them being members of it is considered high, even if it is known that the membership of the category is very small. For instance, if given a description of Joe as impatient, irritable, verbally abusive, and a heavy drinker, a social worker when asked to say whether he is violent or not is likely to say that there is a high probability that he is violent. If the image fits the stereotype of the category, the probability of his being part of it is overestimated. The closer the match between the individual's description and the stereotype, the greater the confidence with which the prediction is made.

In drawing conclusions about the probability of an event people are also willing to base massive generalizations on very small samples. So, for instance, they are willing to extrapolate from two or three examples of violent incidents to the probability of such events generally. They tend to ignore information about the representativeness of the events, and their conclusions also seem to fail to take account of chance variability. They are willing to generalize from one event without recognizing that it may be a completely atypical random occurrence.

Each of these three major biases in estimates of probability will influence the perception of risk. Calculations of their impact cannot be made with any certainty because in reality they push and pull simultaneously in different directions: some promote overestimation, some underestimation of risk. Since accurate risk calculation is vital when trying to cope with violence in the caring professions, individual practitioners need to make themselves aware of the sorts of biases which characterize their estimates. For instance, ask yourself:

- What stereotypes of violent people do you hold?
- What sorts of people do you expect to be violent?
- How surprised would you be if someone without these characteristics were violent towards you?
- What preconceptions do you have about the level of risk you personally are at?
- Is it once a year, once a month, once a week that you are at risk?
- How often do you revise your estimates of risk?
- How frequently do you face a potentially violent situation?
- Is your estimate of your own risk level being influenced by recent examples of dangerous situations you have been in or heard about?

You should try to answer these questions. The object is simply to get to grips with your own personal background considerations which will influence your estimates of risk.

There is one further form of bias worth mentioning here. Familiarity with a situation appears to breed confidence and to reduce perceived risks. People familiar with a situation develop a sense of subjective immunity from its dangers. Even when they recognize the risks at some general, in principle, level for other people, they still regard themselves to be invulnerable. This pattern of risk perception has been found in many contexts. Farmers living on flood plains, even though they knew other farms had been flooded and destroyed, still stayed and argued that it would never happen to them. Smokers, knowing the risks of cancer and cardio-vascular disease, continue to argue that they won't suffer. Those living next to nuclear power plants reckon the risks of radiation are less than do those living further afield. Similarly, members of the caring professions who face dangerous situations regularly are likely to minimize the risks involved. This can, of course, be a way of handling fear by denying danger. It is, however, counterproductive since it may hinder the anticipation and evasion of violence. The point to emphasize is that perceptions of personal risk may not equate with perceptions of the risk faced by others. The sense of subjective immunity is something which most practitioners must curb in the interests of accurately understanding the nature of their relationship with their clients, patients or pupils.

CHAPTER SUMMARY

❏ If you can predict aggression you are in a better position to cope with it. There is evidence that indicates that the risk of violence is greater if: the person belongs to a sub-culture which values or accepts aggression, has a history of violence, is disinhibited or aroused by aversive stimuli, expects violence to be rewarded, or believes no other action is possible.

❏ The risk of physical violence is greater if the person is being verbally abusive, is threatening you, or is emitting nonverbal cues to violence (for example, unusual eye contact, restlessness, clenching fists).

❏ Trigger factors for violence include: intensification of the aversive stimulation; cues which represent violence; verbal provocation; and emergence of new stressors.

❏ The *Dangerousness Checklist* is an aide-mémoire summarizing the risk factors.

❏ Predictors tend to result in over-estimation of risk.

❏ Risk calculations are biased by various heuristics which people employ when processing information: availability, anchoring and adjustment, and representativeness. Subjective immunity assumptions lead people to under-estimate their own vulnerability.

Chapter Four

Patterns of Assault

INCIDENCE OF AGGRESSION

Any estimate of the frequency with which carers face aggression or violence needs to be treated with caution, as there are very few comprehensive surveys of assaults against practitioners. The majority of studies which have examined rates and forms of assault have been restricted to single professional groups and have involved relatively small samples in restricted geographical areas. In summarizing the information available on incidence rates, it is therefore necessary to build up a picture of what happens from a lot of different pockets of data. An additional difficulty is that the definitions of aggression and violence differ across studies – one study will examine only physical assault which has led to injury; another will include everything from verbal abuse onwards. Information from different studies can rarely be compared directly.

Studies also differ in the methods used to collect information. Some rely on administrative records of reported incidents; others employ interviews with random or specific samples of practitioners; and others use large scale questionnaire surveys. These different data collection methods give rise to different conclusions about rates of violence, and it is not at all clear which estimates are most valid. The figures presented here will give you a general impression of the types and extent of assaults.

There is evidence that in the health services one in every 200 staff suffers a major injury following a violent attack each year. A further one in 10 needs first aid and one in 20 is threatened with a knife, chair, broken bottle, and such like. As many as one in six will report being threatened verbally. Most types of serious incidents are more frequent in psychiatric facilities. In such settings, one in four staff members reports suffering minor injury after attacks. In geriatric and psychiatric hospitals, the comparable figure is one in five. The staff who are most vulnerable across settings are student nurses and ambulance drivers. These figures probably underestimate the scale of the problem since many assaults go unreported.

These rates can be compared with those collated by the police for violence to the general public: the incidence rate for serious wounding is about one in 5,300 for males; one in 25,000 for females. For less serious wounding, the rates are approximately one in 310 and one in 880 respectively. If these estimates are taken seriously, it seems that health service workers are at least 26 times more likely to be seriously injured than members of the general public, and the increase in risk is greater for female health workers. The general figures may be considered an inappropriate basis for comparison since they are gross estimates, but even when other comparators are chosen the picture looks unhealthy. The rate of serious injury in the health service is twice as high as in the construction industry and five times as high as in the manufacturing sector.

In the social services the picture is hardly better. According to official statistics, in urban areas, one in 130 staff members in a year reports assaults; in rural areas the rate drops to one in 434 staff. There is a disparity in the rates for fieldworkers and residential workers – for fieldworkers it works out at about one in 372, for residential workers it is one in 228. However, the official figures are consistently shown to under-represent actual violence when compared with the results of intensive studies. These suggest that around one in 25 per annum experience an attack which results in injury requiring medical assistance, and roughly one third of these injuries is moderately serious or severe. The rate of verbal abuse and threat is immense. Some studies have reported that as many as 96 per cent of staff in social services offices will be abused in the course of a two-month period. Ninety-three per cent will have threats of violence, 67 per cent will have threats backed with a weapon, 83 per cent will experience actual violence, and 41 per cent will have to face violence with a weapon.

The situation for teachers in schools is surprisingly similar. Approximately one in four is threatened with violence and one in 10 will suffer an attempted attack each year; one in 25 suffers actual physical violence.

Large-scale studies have revealed that 50 per cent of teachers regard indiscipline as a frequent or regular occurrence in the classroom. One in three experiences major disruption in their class in a year. One in five reports physical violence, though not always directed at themselves. Most attacks are by pupils on teachers, though as many as 10 per cent will be verbally or physically attacked by parents of pupils.

ECOLOGY OF AGGRESSION

Each violent incident is undoubtedly unique. However, there are some patterns which emerge for the caring professions. For instance, in social services, residential workers tend to be assaulted by males; fieldworkers are mostly assaulted by females. Female fieldworkers are very rarely assaulted by a man. The worst affected locations were old people's homes and adolescent treatment centres. Most incidents occur in communal areas at times when the officer in charge was off duty. Many assaults involve repeat incidents with the same carer being attacked by the same client. The assaults virtually never occur on first contact with the social worker. Half the social workers attacked would rate the relationship with the assailant before the attack as good. As many as 85 per cent of assaults are committed by established clients whom the social worker has known for some time. Around 10 per cent of assaults are perpetrated by a member of the client's family rather than the actual client. Attacks tend to take place in the client's primary or secondary territory, which means in the home or, in the case of institutionalized clients, in areas where they feel some sense of possession or control. Social workers were most vulnerable in their cars, then in clients' homes, and then in social work offices.

Interestingly, given what was said earlier about frustration and pain as a cause of violence, the places where most attacks take place in the health service are hospital emergency and accident departments. Initially, it is rather difficult to compare the violence teachers may face with that experienced by other practitioners. Evidence of the psychological or social profile of pupil attackers is not available, nor is information on the specific context or background to attacks available. We do need more information on these aspects of violence in schools. Without it, risk estimation is virtually impossible.

TYPES OF VIOLENCE

The physical assault is almost always preceded by verbal abuse or threats. The form which it takes depends greatly upon the context in which it occurs, the relative physical strength of the participants and the nature of the trigger for the attack. Practitioners expect to face, in descending likelihood of occurrence: pushing, holding, kicking, punching, hair-pulling, stabbing, and strangulation. Sexual assault is considered unlikely. By and large, the limited evidence available confirms these expectations.

PHYSICAL CONCOMITANTS OF AGGRESSION

To understand the typical pattern of events in an assault, it is useful to be aware of the physical changes which are occurring at the time. Aggression is typically accompanied by physiological changes in the attacker and attacked which are virtually identical. The overt symptoms of these physical changes can be used to improve the assessment of risk. If you sense these changes occurring in yourself, you should pay attention to them. Your body is telling you that you are afraid. Fear is information for you to use. It is a good indication that there is something threatening in the situation, even if professionally you wish to ignore it.

When danger or threat is perceived, the adrenal glands are triggered by the hypothalamus in the brain to secrete a chemical called *adrenaline* into the bloodstream. This hormone has the following effects:

- glucose is released to help muscles work more efficiently;
- breathing gets quicker so oxygen can transform glucose into energy;
- the heart beats faster to take extra oxygen in the blood to the muscles, and increases blood pressure;
- blood is diverted from the digestive system to compensate, with symptoms of nausea and dry mouth;
- muscles tense for action;
- skin changes occur, sweating cools the body, the face may pale as blood is diverted to the muscles;
- the pupils dilate to make vision clearer.

Once the danger has passed, the adrenal glands secrete another hormone called noradrenalin. This serves to counteract the effects of the adrenaline. These are powerful chemicals and they often leave after-effects such as:

- a sense of emptiness and disorientation;
- feelings of depression and lack of vitality;

- a sense of anti-climax (especially if no action was taken);
- mild confusion;
- headaches;
- physical weakness.

The physiological peak and trough of the aggressive encounter is thought to be echoed in a cognitive, behavioural and emotional cycle known as the *Assault Cycle*.

THE ASSAULT CYCLE

Situational analyses of acts of violence have resulted in researchers asserting that an act of violence is part of a cycle of behaviour: the Assault Cycle. The structure of the Assault Cycle has been described following the analysis of hundreds of accounts of incidents of violence. A series of interrelated phases is typically found in most assault situations.

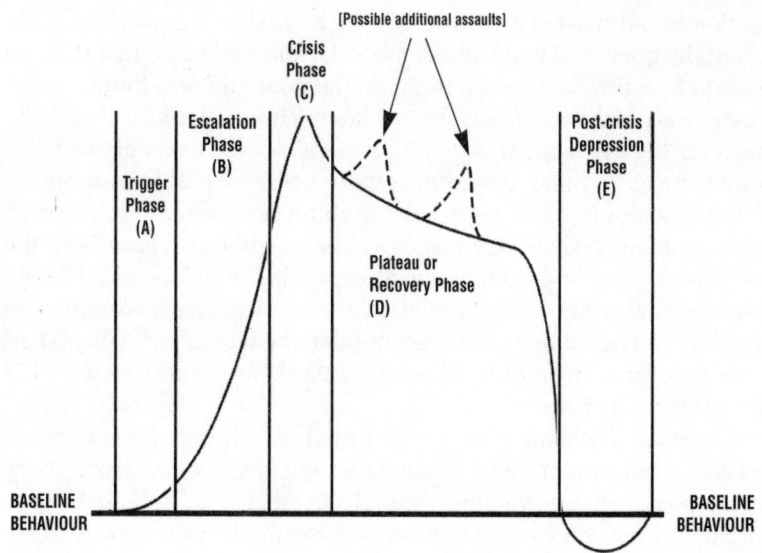

Figure 1: THE TYPICAL ASSAULT CYCLE

THE TRIGGER PHASE

Irrespective of setting, people have a normal baseline set of behaviours, and for almost everyone this normal behaviour is non-aggressive for most of the time. The trigger phase is the point at which the individual first indicates a movement away from how they usually behave. Such changes may be perceived in nonverbal or verbal behaviour; for example, in unwillingness to sit down, inability to wait for you to complete your sentences, answering before questions are completed, failing to make eye contact, and so on. The less detailed understanding you have of a particular individual, the more easily you can miss these early warning signs of the possibility of an attack or violent outburst.

The actual triggers which cue this phase vary greatly. For instance, in geriatric residential settings, the trigger can be a by-product of audio-visual handicaps which lead to misunderstanding and suspicion. Lack of space and privacy are also identified as major triggers for violence. Alcohol, drugs (prescription or otherwise), and tiredness are additional well-established triggers. Resistance to staff handling or attention also represent frequent triggers. Receipt of bad news can be a trigger. For some people, particular words or labels stimulate aggression. For instance, Sybil, an 87-year-old woman who was blind and crippled with arthritis, was being assessed by a social worker for admission into hospital. She had fallen the previous night when she got out of bed to go to the toilet and had been unable to get back to bed. She had lain all night on the floor and was found by her next-door-neighbour many hours later. This had precipitated the need for the assessment. A young female social worker arrived and found the old woman uncommunicative. She would not respond to direct questioning and kept talking about her cats. After about 45 minutes the social worker turned to the neighbour who was in the room with them and said, 'Is she always this cantankerous?' The old woman hurled her walking stick at the social worker, wheezing as she did so, 'I heard that'. It turned out that the woman's husband had been fond of accusing her of being cantankerous and had deserted her many years before.

The main problem with triggers or flashpoints is their idiosyncrasy. Within a potentially violent situation, the possible triggers are numerous. You are walking through an uncharted minefield. You might be very lucky and get through unscathed, but it is more likely that you will land upon one.

THE ESCALATION PHASE

This phase leads directly to the violent behaviour. The individual's behaviour deviates more and more from its baseline level. If there is no intervention, the deviation will become both increasingly more obvious and less amenable to diversion. For instance, the person may start to pace up and down, the speed of their speech may increase, as may the volume, and your queries may be ignored completely. The individual is likely to become overly focused on a particular issue and is less likely to respond to any form of rational intervention. It is therefore important to intervene as early as possible in the escalation phase by, for example, counselling, removal from the immediate environment, or supplying an alternative task, or even the provision of anger-management techniques.

During this phase, your own actions are likely to be over-interpreted and your posture and stance will be perceived as aggressive. For instance, raising your arms or standing with your hands on your hips will be read as challenging or offensive. Your eye contact will be seen as aggressive, 'staring down' and confrontational. Essentially, the assailant is looking for any cue to justify the attack.

Let us go back to the case of Sybil. The social worker picked up the stick and, rubbing her arm which had been scratched by the blow, turned to the old woman and told her that such behaviour was unnecessary. The young social worker thought her tone was pleasant and inoffensive, but Sybil subsequently described it as 'Sounding like this little kid was lecturing me, in my own home. People think because you are blind you can't tell when they are patronizing you'. The social worker compounded the incitement by asking if Sybil was still able to look after her cats, as there seemed to be rather a lot of them. Sybil thought this was an accusation that the cats were maltreated and told the young woman to leave. The social worker would not go while Sybil was so clearly upset. Sybil became angrier and started to lash out indiscriminately with the walking stick which had been returned to her. The neighbour told the social worker to go out and she calmed Sybil down. Sybil subsequently refused to allow any social worker in the house.

THE CRISIS PHASE

As the individual becomes increasingly physically, emotionally and psychologically aroused, control over aggressive impulses lessens and actual violent behaviour becomes more likely. For example, kicking or overturning furniture, pushing or punching the practitioner, throwing crockery, are all common. In this phase, the least effective strategy is to adopt an intervention which presumes that the individual can respond rationally. Any attempt at verbal argument or confrontation from you is likely to exaggerate the agitation of the assailant. Once the crisis phase has been reached, it is advisable to focus on your own safety and the safety of your client or anyone else who may be threatened. Attempts to hold or touch the assailant are extremely dangerous at this stage and may precipitate more extreme aggression. The options available to you may be very limited: to escape the situation, to engage in physical restraint, to seek help by whatever means are available, or physically to protect yourself from the individual by imposing barriers. By this phase, the assailant will normally have persuaded themselves that the attack is justified and unavoidable.

THE RECOVERY PHASE

The individual will gradually return to normal baseline behaviour once the violent act has occurred. It is at this point that most intervention errors occur. The individual's high state of physical and psychological arousal can remain for a period of up to one and a half hours after the incident itself. Attempts at intervention in this period can result in the renewal of the violent attack. In fact, it appears that, during the recovery phase, the individual is particularly sensitive to the sorts of trigger factors which have been described earlier.

An example of the dangers of the recovery phase arose in a hostel for homeless people. Lacey, a 52-year-old alcoholic with a history of psychiatric hospitalization, had been refused a bed for the night by a young female volunteer worker at the hostel, largely because on a previous visit she had broken up the kitchen whilst hallucinating after a bad drinking binge. Lacey stood outside the hostel shouting and throwing bricks at the light above the door. After half an hour or so, the volunteer, who was alone in the hostel, called the police. Their arrival precipitated Lacey into a frantic attack on the door and windows of the hostel. Bricks flew everywhere, hitting a police officer accidentally. The police finally subdued Lacey and she was taken inside the hostel, appearing to become calmer. She was left alone in the kitchen with the volunteer for a few minutes once she settled down. She drank some tea and the volunteer assumed that she was stabilized since she appeared completely calm. At this point, the volunteer said that Lacey must leave, since no bed was available. Without warning, Lacey smashed her mug on the table and rammed the broken shards into the volunteer's face.

This phenomenon of a sudden step-change in aggression during the 'recovery phase' is something to watch for closely. It is dangerous because the assailant does not retrace the path through the trigger and escalation phases which would offer you time to think and scope for management.

POST-CRISIS DEPRESSION PHASE

In the post-crisis depression phase, the individual often regresses below normal baseline behaviour. Mental and physical exhaustion are common, precipitated by the physiological changes described earlier, and the individual may become tearful, remorseful, guilty, ashamed, distraught or despairing. The crisis is over and the individual may be receptive to interventions designed to relieve guilt, understand the incident, and perhaps prevent its recurrence.

In the descriptions given, the phases of the Assault Cycle have been depicted in terms of how they are experienced on the part of the aggressor. It should be emphasized that there is evidence to support the argument that the individual having to deal with the potential aggressor (often the potential victim) experiences a similar set of phases during the assault cycle. During the escalation phase, the potential victim has a considerable increase in arousal levels which peak during the crisis phase. This means that at precisely the moment when it is important for the potential victim to behave in a rational and effective manner, the heightening of psychological and physical arousal is likely to hamper both the practitioner's control and effectiveness. During the recovery phase, the practitioner is similarly likely to echo the experiences of the aggressor, and the practitioner and potential victim is likely to be easily tipped into excessive anxiety or even excessive hilarity as a consequence of physiological arousal during the recovery phase. In the post-crisis depression phase, the practitioner will feel parallel exhaustion or fatigue to that experienced by the aggressor. Given that this is the case, it is particularly difficult for the practitioner who has experienced the attack to cope with the organization and provision of the interventions necessary for the client during this phase.

The Assault Cycle is a useful tool for schematizing a process which occurs during a typical episode of aggressive behaviour. This analysis emphasizes that intervention is possible at all times, except in the crisis phase, when the practitioner should consider his or her own physical safety and that of the client paramount. The analysis indicates that both the aggressor and the practitioner experience high levels of physical or psychological arousal during episodes of aggressive behaviour, and this will affect how they both behave. The practitioner must develop techniques to overcome this.

Finally, the analysis suggests that most violent incidents are understandable and can be prevented or at least ameliorated with the correct interventions at the appropriate time.

AGGRESSION PREFERENCES

In attempting to understand patterns of assault, it is useful to recognize that people differ in the preferences they evolve for different forms of expressing their aggression. The Aggression Preferences assessment exercise allows you to explore your own preferred styles of aggression. It is certainly worth knowing this, since these preferences will affect how you respond in an attack situation. The assessment yields four scores. The first indicates whether you prefer verbal rather than physical aggression. The second indexes whether you displace your aggression from its original source. The third measures whether you feel you remain calm whilst being aggressive. The fourth indicates whether you direct your aggression inwards, against yourself, or target it outwards, towards others. The assessment merely focuses your attention on these facets of your aggression – your natural or habitual preferences may not be the most effective or advisable. Certainly avoiding intrapunitive and displaced aggression is probably sensible, since both forms of aggression merely compound the effects of the original attack: hurting yourself or others who are innocent is not productive. Fostering calm, verbal responses is probably productive. The assessment may also provide you with a framework for analysing the aggression preferences of other people, especially clients. Trying to anticipate behaviour on the basis of revealed preferences is worth attempting and it is yet another technique which will improve your assessment of risks and your capacity to evolve management strategies.

SELF-ASSESSMENT EXERCISE 4
AGGRESSION PREFERENCES

This exercise is designed to help you assess what forms of aggression or violence you are personally likely to exhibit. You may already have a good understanding of your own responses when angry, but this set of questions is designed to illustrate the range of potential responses and indicate how your own pattern relates to it. For each statement, put a tick in the column which best reflects the frequency with which you respond in that way.

When angry, I am the sort of person who:

Usually   Sometimes   Never

1. Becomes cool and deliberately self-controlled.

2. Remains calm.

3. Becomes verbally vicious.

4. Becomes speechless.

5. Tries to leave the situation or person generating the anger.

6. Wants to hurt someone else.

7. Uses physical attacks on the cause of the anger so as to eliminate it.

8. Becomes annoyed with myself.

9. Feels very guilty.

10. Yells or screams.

11. Cries.

12. Flies into a rage.

13. Bottles up the feeling and finds some outlet for it later.

continued

continued _____

14. Fails to tackle the cause of the
     anger directly.

15. Thinks about and analyses the angering
     experience for a long time after.

16. Cannot resist making threatening
     gestures at the person who angers me.

17. Punishes the person who angers me by
     withdrawing my affection or respect.

18. Loses control of myself.

19. Redirects the anger towards inanimate
     objects (e.g. kicking the furniture).

20. Allows my anger to show in my general
     demeanor.

These questions tap four dimensions along which aggression
may be expressed:

Verbal ——————————————————— Physical

This reflects the self-evident distinction between the expression of anger in words or in actions. It is worth emphasizing that the two blend together at points and the same person can use both forms of aggression at different times. It is nevertheless the case that you will have expressed something about how frequently you engage in both sorts. The important thing to establish is your preferred or habitual mode. Items 3, 4, 10, 16, and 17 index this dimension. For items 3, 10 and 17 score 3 for 'usually', 2 for 'sometimes', and 1 for 'never'; for items 4 and 16, score 3 for 'never', 2 for 'sometimes', and 1 for 'usually'. The higher your score, the more you use verbal expressions of aggression and avoid physical aggression. NB: If you score 2 across all five items you are using both verbal and physical styles of aggression.

_____ *continued*

continued -

Direct ————————————————————— Displaced

This represents the less obvious distinction between aggression which is directed at the reason for your anger and that which is displaced onto other objects. This is 'kick the cat instead of the boss' phenomenon. Displacement can occur for many reasons: fear or concern for the real object of your anger being the prime causes. Items 5, 7, 13, 14 and 19 index the tendency to displacement. Score 3 for 'usually', 2 for 'sometimes', 1 for 'never' on items 5, 13, 14, and 19; reverse the scoring for item 7. The greater your score, the higher the level of displacement you engage in.

Fury ———————————————————————— Calm

This reflects the level of self-control you believe you have when angry. People differ in the extent to which they allow anger to be translated into passion. Some, when angry, become calculating and cold. Items 1, 2, 12, 18, and 20 refer to this facet of the expression of aggression. Items 1 and 2 should be scored 3 for 'usually', 2 for 'sometimes', 1 for 'never'; scoring for items 12, 18, and 20 is reversed. The higher the score, the greater the level of calmness.

Intra-punitive ————————————————— Extra-punitive

This refers to the direction of aggression. Intra-punitive responses entail directing the aggression inwards, against yourself. Extra-punitive responses entail externalizing the aggression. Self-blame, self-doubt, shame and guilt can all be forms of intra-punitiveness. Intra-punitiveness has also been linked with various psychosomatic complaints such asthma and stomach ulcers. Items 6, 8, 9, 11 and 15 are designed to tap the extent of intra-punitiveness. Score 3 for 'usually', 2 for 'sometimes' and 1 for 'never' on items 8, 9, 11, and 15; scoring for item 6 is reversed. A higher score indicates higher intra-punitiveness.

There are currently no standard scores for the caring professions against which you could compare yourself on these indices. If you want to compare your own responses with those of others in your professional group, you could get some of your colleagues to go through the exercise too.

CHAPTER SUMMARY

❏ There is only limited evidence on the incidence of assaults on practitioners. That which exists indicates that carers face violence leading to minor or severe physical injury significantly more frequently than other occupational groups. Verbal abuse and threats are virtually an everyday occurrence for the majority.

❏ Data on violence against social workers indicates that residential workers are mostly assaulted by males; fieldworkers are most attacked by females. Repeat assaults are common. Established clients are more likely to be violent than new contacts. In the health services, aggressive incidents are most frequent in emergency and accident departments.

❏ The physical concomitants of threat, controlled by the secretion of adrenalin, entail increases in muscle tension, blood pressure, and oxygen, glucose and blood supply to the muscles. The body is readied for flight or fight. Once the danger passes, the after-effects of this bodily reaction can be serious: confusion, headaches, depression, and physical weakness.

❏ Violence is part of a cycle of behaviour: the *Assault Cycle,* which involves five phases (the trigger, escalation, crisis, recovery and post-crisis depression phases). The Assault Cycle applies equally to the assailant and the victim. Knowing about it allows you to better predict the development of violent incidents and to understand your own reactions to them.

❏ People differ in their preferences for different forms of aggression. Knowing your own preferences allows you to understand better what you may want to do should you be attacked.

Chapter Five

Victims and Victimization

CHARACTERISTICS OF THE VICTIMS

Before you go any further, complete the 'Victims of Attack' assessment exercise which follows. It asks you to outline which qualities you think characterize practitioners who are assaulted by the people they work with (for example, clients, patients, pupils). Try to be completely honest in the responses that you record – you are your only audience. Open your mind to your own beliefs and, indeed, to your own prejudices. We all carry around expectations about the type of practitioner who gets attacked. These amount to simple stereotypes of victims. Social psychologists define a stereotype as a set of characteristics which are attributed to all members of a particular category purely on the basis of their membership of that category. For instance, you might hold a stereotype of all accountants as money-grabbing, small-minded, picky, gray individuals. If so, the mere fact that someone is known to be an accountant would result in you expecting that she or he would exhibit those characteristics. The 'Victims of Attack' assessment exercise is designed to allow you to confront your own stereotypes.

Rowett (1986), in the most comprehensive survey of violence against social workers to date, showed that social workers themselves seemed to believe that other social workers who were assaulted were more provocative, incompetent, authoritarian and inexperienced. They were felt to seek out risky situations, confront clients and challenge them unnecessarily, and also were thought to be more demanding, less flexible and less able to detect potentially dangerous situations. It is fascinating that Rowett found that the assaulted social workers *themselves* shared this set of beliefs about the characteristics

SELF-ASSESSMENT EXERCISE 5:
VICTIMS OF ATTACKS

Simply record your answers to the following questions and then compare them with what you subsequently learn from the research which is summarized in this chapter. Check whether your beliefs parallel those of other practitioners.

Rate practitioners who are assaulted by their clients by the extent to which you think they are likely to have the following characteristics.

	Extremely	Very	Quite	Not much	Not at all
Liberal					
Dogmatic					
Authoritarian					
Gentle					
Provocative					
Strong					
Willing to take risks					
Experienced					
Competent					
Insightful					

typifying victims of attack. This must be compared with their equally forcefully expressed belief that their own assaults were never purely their own fault.

It is notable in the light of this stereotype of the assaulted social worker that when Rowett's respondents completed an objective standardized test designed to measure hostility levels, all fell within the normal range and there were no differences between residential or field workers or between assaulted and non-assaulted. There seems little firm evidence for the pervasive stereotype concerning the attitudes and skill-deficits of those who are attacked.

Interestingly, the stereotype did not extend to sex and physique as predisposing factors for assault. On this there was no consistent pattern in the attitudes expressed: some considered women to be more at risk, others thought men more open to attack; some thought small stature an incitement to attack, others felt the big and strong were fairer game. Again, the important thing is that there is no real evidence to support either set of beliefs. The stereotypes are based on a heavy concoction of wishful-thinking, denial, and prejudice, but certainly not on evidence. It is worth noting that the stereotype is damningly negative and might be expected to affect the way a victim of attack handles the experience. It may go some way to accounting for the failures to report incidents (estimates of more than 60 per cent of victims failing to report an assault are common). It may also account for some of the reticence on the part of managers to provide support for victims who are seen, in part at least, as the originators of their own problem.

The truth of the matter is that *anyone* can be the victim of an assault; there is no evidence that victims share some common set of characteristics. At least, if they do share characteristics, they are the opposite of those assumed in the stereotype. Those who are assaulted are found to be:

- experienced with no record of incompetence;
- not risk takers and sensitive to cues in situations where they work;
- not confrontational or particularly provocative or authoritarian;
- physically capable and decisive in their actions.

The stereotype is misleading and counterproductive, and if you believe it you would be wise to abandon it **now**.

TYPICAL REACTIONS TO ASSAULT

Consider what you would do and how you would feel in the following situation:

❏ You are a health visitor and upon a visit to the house of a young woman with a new baby, you are accused of interference by the woman's lover because you point out that the child is not gaining weight at the expected rate. You explain that you are trying to help. He becomes angry and starts shouting. The young woman intervenes to quiet him but he pushes her aside and starts to slap her. You then try to get between them and grab his arm, pushing him backwards. He switches his attack to you. You are bruised and your lip is cut before his attack subsides and you are able to escape.

Now make a note of what you think you would do, say and feel. After reading the rest of this chapter, do this again and compare your answers. You could then consider how you would handle the victim of the assault if you were their line manager or senior colleague.

The reactions following an assault are well-documented. It is useful to know how people commonly react to assault, especially if you have to deal with the effects yourself. It is reassuring sometimes to know that the way in which you are reacting is not unique or in some way wrong or unexpected. Unfortunately, there is actually very little evidence about the effects which assault specifically has upon practitioners. There is anecdotal information, but any generalizations must be based upon what we know of the effects of violent assault upon other victims. The response seems to have a number of stages, two of which, the Crisis phase and the Post-crisis Depression, comprise the final phases of the Assault Cycle described in the last chapter.

STAGES OF RESPONSE TO ASSAULT

1. Crisis Phase – lasting up to 90 minutes after the assault. Adrenaline will still be pumping, tension gradually abates but is followed by physical and mental exhaustion. This is exemplified by the case of one nurse who was able to finish her night duty after being punched several times while restraining a drunk in the accident department, but the following day found herself lethargic and incapable of coping with even the simplest task.

2. Post-Crisis Depression – the assault is often interpreted as dehumanizing and degrading. In the case of practitioners, depression is often focused upon the loss of confidence in ability to handle any client and the loss of the sense of vocation or professional identity. Depression of this sort is often associated with sleeplessness and a pervasive sense of hopelessness.

3. Medium Term Effects – overestimating the likelihood of subsequent violence. In the case of practitioners, this may be manifested in disproportionate fear of clients/patients/pupils with a violent record or of situations where violence is likely; wariness of any new situation or new contacts; no longer being willing to confront people because they are unwilling to face any real risk to themselves; becoming very apprehensive when people approach from behind. One young teacher, who had been locked in a cupboard for two hours by a bunch of pupils who threatened to burn him alive after he had intervened to stop a fight, explained that he had resigned and gone to another school because he never felt safe again in that school's precincts. For him the change of schools had little effect – he remained fearful of his charges and finally left the profession.

4. Longer Term Effects – being unexpectedly overwhelmed with fear when re-living the traumatic event in the form of intrusive memories or flashbacks and succumbing to denial of the incident or attempting to erase the feelings associated with it. The effects of an assault may continue to be felt months or even years later, and in some cases, long after the physical scars have healed. In this sense, it has much in common with any traumatic stressful event.

In their most complete manifestations, the effects of assault will equate to the symptoms of Post-Traumatic Stress Disorder (PTSD). PTSD is defined by the American Psychiatric Association as the development of characteristic symptoms following exposure to an extreme traumatic stressor which evokes intense fear, helplessness or horror. These symptoms include: the persistent re-experience of the event in one or more of a series of ways – as recurrent distressing recollections, dreams or sense of recurrence of the event; and physiological and psychological distress when exposed to cues symbolizing or resembling the event. Normally this leads to persistent avoidance of stimuli associated with the trauma (including anything remotely likely to arouse recollections) and the numbing of general responsiveness (lowered emotionality, foreshortening of aspirations about the future). Simultaneously, there is persistent evidence of increased arousal: difficulty in sleeping; irritability and angry outbursts; difficulty in concentration; hypervigilance; exaggerated startle response.

Someone evincing these symptoms for three months or more is said to have chronic PTSD.

HANDLING THE EFFECTS

It would be a mistake to suppose that the stages in the reaction to any serious assault could be subverted or easily curtailed. The most sensible self-help strategy is to seek out as much support from others as you can, in both professional circles and from friends or family. Isolating yourself in the hope of dealing with the reactions in secret may simply intensify them. Of course, seeking help has its costs: the loss of self-esteem, the risk of humiliation or of being blamed as a victim. These will be discussed in more detail later.

The intensity of the reaction will depend on the nature of the attack and the characteristics of the individual. Assaults differ on a number of dimensions: the length of time they last (some only moments, others may last days); the degree of injury inflicted; type of injury (physical/emotional/psychological); and so on. There is no consistent pattern of relationships between the characteristics of the assault and the reactions it elicits. The effect of the characteristics of the individual upon response seems more predictable. In their negative reactions to assault, people seem to exaggerate tendencies they already have. So, for instance, the previously anxious person becomes more anxious; the depressed slips into greater depression.

The longevity of the effects will also depend upon the immediate manner in which the incident is handled. Failure by managers to debrief staff who have been involved in an attack may leave the victim with no means of exploring the meaning of the event with someone who understands the nature of the job. The failure to provide an arena in which the incident can be analysed and interpreted is likely to prolong the time it takes the individual to come to terms with it.

FEAR, SURPRISE, ANGER AND GUILT

Rowett (1986) showed that the immediate emotional response to assault is fear, followed by surprise and then anger. But upon the heels of anger comes guilt. This seems to stem from a number of sources.

The assaulted practitioners, though mostly feeling that the incident was unpredictable, believed it to be understandable and presumably in some senses justified. While not thinking the incident to be their own fault, neither did they consider it to be the client's fault alone. Instead the majority considered both themselves and the client to be at fault. Guilt can be the product of self-blame even if the victim is unwilling to shoulder the entire responsibility. This pattern of results is paralleled in smaller ethnographic studies in schools and hospitals.

The assaulted often think that it is some failing in their professional skills which has made them incapable of de-fusing the violent situation and preventing the attack. This idea is succoured by the rhetoric which suggests that once you have been on a training course in handling violence all will be well. It is further supported by the tendency for senior colleagues to keep quiet about their own experiences of violence.

Guilt is sometimes generated after the practitioner is attacked more than once. In fact, it seems to be the case that some people are assaulted relatively frequently. In their cases, it may seem a reasonable conclusion that it is something about them which incites attack: their attitude or ineptitude and guilt might seem appropriate. Of course, such a conclusion may be totally unjustified – it may just be that they work in particularly high risk areas.

The guilt response is common in many traumatically stressful incidents. For instance, survivors of tragedies where others have died often feel guilt despite being innocent of any responsibility for the disaster. The guilt of victims may be a symptom of stress rather than any rational evaluation of responsibility for the event.

Guilt is a debilitating response, and it often leads to self-doubt and blame. These in turn destroy confidence and authority. Practice becomes a nightmare. Sometimes the loss of confidence spreads out from the victim to colleagues. A community team leader working in social services in an Outer London borough described what happened to her team after she was assaulted by a client whom she was trying to move from home into a hostel. She said that the team was shattered, and the main problem for her as team leader was the loss of authority and the threat posed to the junior members of the team when they recognized that their leader was vulnerable. As she said, 'If I can't protect myself, how can I expect to protect them?' The practitioner sometimes feels guilty not just for having been assaulted, but for the incipient threat posed to colleagues.

It may be unrealistic to expect to get over the emotional aftermath of an attack without professional help. Carers have a tendency to avoid using the services of other carers, but in this case, seeking counselling help may be productive, particularly immediately after the incident. Counselling might focus upon the irrationality and damaging impact of guilt.

DETERMINANTS OF VICTIM REACTIONS

Victims differ in the extent to which they exhibit adverse post-trauma reactions, but it is possible to profile those who are at greatest risk of the most severe effects.

● Someone who is dealing with other significant stressors prior to the incident is more likely to find it hard to cope with the aftermath of the assault. If someone is suffering a physical illness, domestic conflict or career difficulties before the attack, dealing with the attack will be more difficult. The psychological effects of stressors are in a crude fashion cumulative.

● Those with depressive tendencies are more likely to perceive the assault as part of a series of events, uncontrollable and leading to generally dire consequences. This mind set makes it difficult for them to put the specific incident into perspective and a one-off problem is construed as a constant threat.

● People who lack social support networks (such as good friends, a sympathetic spouse or other relatives) with whom they can discuss how they feel about the incident fare less well than those who have such support.

● People who strongly believe the 'blaming' stereotype of victims tend to react worse after an assault than those who reject the stereotype.

● People who derive their self-esteem largely or solely from their perception of themselves as a practitioner often suffer badly after an assault since the attack represents a major blow to their source of positive feelings about themselves.

It is useful to know something of the personal determinants of variation in the severity of reactions to an assault as it can help to decide the form that any assistance should take. For instance, you might need to enhance the person's support network; alternatively, you may be better advised to offer information which breaks down stereotyped opinions about victims or bolsters self-esteem by showing they are not professionally inept.

VICTIMIZATION

The self-blame and guilt which follow an assault may be exacerbated by any stereotypes held by the caring professions. It has already been argued that social workers share the belief that colleagues who are attacked are provocative, inexperienced, authoritarian, incompetent, demanding, inflexible and incapable of detecting the signs of violence in a situation. Similar stereotypes are produced by nurses and teachers about the members of their professions who are assaulted. These stereotypes attribute the blame to the victim and they are pictured as different from other practitioners. As I mentioned before, the strange thing is that the assaulted also accept the stereotype. They may not always recognize that it describes themselves personally, but even they are willing to say that other people who get attacked are like that.

This acceptance of a self-deprecating stereotype is a phenomenon which occurs in other contexts. Groups which have little power will accept for themselves the stereotype generated about them by more dominant groups, and will believe that they have those characteristics. There is extensive evidence that before the Black Power Movement, black people in the US accepted the stereotype of them as lazy and stupid but at the same time cunning and childlike. Subordinate groups find it hard to resist the stereotype which acts to legitimize their powerlessness by making them seem less worthy of equality. And the stereotype, once assimilated by a group, can become a self-fulfilling prophesy; individuals in the group begin to act in ways which accord with the expectations of the stereotype.

Any victim who becomes aware of the stereotype will recognize that they are considered responsible for their own fate. This awareness of the beliefs which pervade their own subculture will breed guilt and self-blame. But why should such a stereotype exist? It seems in part to be a manifestation of two biases which are fundamental to the way people explain what happens in the world (Weiner, 1995). The first bias concerns what are called 'actor–observer' differences in attribution (see also p.33). If you watch someone do something and are then asked to explain why they did it, you are most likely to produce an explanation in terms of the characteristics of the person (their motives, personality, background, and so on). If you do something yourself and are asked to explain it, you are most likely to generate some explanation in terms of situational constraints or circumstances. This is the actor–observer difference in its simplest form. When applied to the interpretation of a violent incident, this bias in interpretation will lead to explanations in terms of the characteristics of the assailant and the victim, rather than in terms of the situation or the broader societal framework.

The second bias concerns the *Just World Hypothesis*. This focuses upon the idea that people believe that there is a match between what people do and what happens to them. In explaining events, people seem to suppose that people only get what is coming to them. If something bad happens to you, it is assumed that you must have deserved it. At some level there seems to be some notion that celestial retribution is at work. The *Just World Hypothesis* results in the victims of crime, for instance, being seen in some way as the originators of their own fate. They are consequently subject to censure, not sympathy.

Most of the research in this area has involved getting people to explain a rape or a mugging or some other violent crime. Most people will attribute responsibility to the victim. The raped woman is likely to have been flirting or to have a history of promiscuity known to the man. The person who was mugged is supposed to have been walking in a dangerous area at the wrong time of day or night. Responsibility for the crime is shifted subtly on to the shoulders of the victim. The stereotyping of the assaulted practitioner is merely the routine extension of this process of victimization: the carer is not thought to have fulfilled the obligations of the caring role properly.

The stereotype may have arisen because of these general biases in information processing and explanation, but it is maintained because it serves a purpose. It serves to locate the control of violence in the practitioner: the violence is not random or fundamentally uncontrollable, it is due to practitioner inadequacies. This is assuring – so long as you are not inadequate, you can expect to remain safe. This stereotype actually protects the majority of practitioners from the truth, which is that anyone can be a victim. People are motivated to accept the stereotype without challenge; to fail to do so would call into question one's own passport to safety.

The existence of the stereotype, and the consequent possibility for victimization probably accounts in large part for the small proportion of violent incidents which is reported. It may also contribute to the difficulties which managers have in providing support for the assaulted after the event. Very few victims report that they receive adequate support from their managers. They describe how their supervisors or managers seem embarrassed about talking about the incident and how, after a very short time, a wall of silence descends. This still seems to be happening, even after the upsurge of publicity about the violence faced by the caring professions and the need for management support.

❑ Case study: Sarah

An example of the more insidious forms of victimization comes from the case of Sarah, who was a probationer teacher in an inner city school which catered for the full academic ability range. Her first three months in the school were highly successful and she enjoyed the variety in her teaching, which ranged from the 11–12 year olds through to 17–18 year olds and encompassed all levels of ability. After the Christmas vacation she took over a class of 15-year-olds who were scheduled to leave school at the end of the year. They were considered the most difficult group in the school and were mainly boys, lacking respect for the teachers and holding little hope that they would be able to get jobs on leaving school. Sarah was assigned to teach them English. One day, while asking them to read and comment on a Shakespeare play, she realized that two of the boys at the back of this class of 34 pupils were trying to molest one of the female pupils. They had sandwiched the girl between them and were trying to feel her breasts and put their hands up her skirt. Sarah told the boys to stop it immediately. They protested that they had done nothing. Sarah told them to come to the front of the class. They refused and one told her to 'Fuck off'. The rest of the class watched in anticipation. The tension was palpable. Sarah went to pull the struggling girl from between the lads, and, in doing so, she overbalanced and fell forward onto the lap of one of the boys. The rest of the class started to laugh and someone said 'Never mind the girl, teacher wants some herself'. The lads, laughing, started to push Sarah onto the floor. She slapped one across the face and at that moment a male teacher who had heard the noise from an adjoining room came in. He got Sarah out of the room and ordered the culprits to the head teacher.

Sarah was not physically injured by the incident. She did, however, find it difficult to go into school the next day and felt that when she walked through the playground everyone was laughing at her. Her head teacher said nothing to her about the incident after the initial report was made, and no attempt was made to debrief her. Other colleagues avoided the topic and she overheard on two occasions more experienced colleagues suggest that probationer teachers were simply not trained nowadays to deal with difficult pupils. One said to her that she should never raise a hand to pupils. When it came to the scheduled meeting with the same class the next week, she was unable to face them. She used the excuse that she had bad toothache and had to go to the dentist. Her head teacher did not question her about this co-incidence, although subsequently it became obvious that he had noted the fact. Sarah's teaching performance was affected by the incident. She did not like to move around the classroom, and stayed as much as possible behind her desk. She avoided direct confrontation with pupils and discipline in her classrooms was poor. Within three weeks, Sarah had decided that she could not teach in that school any longer.

It was at this point that the process of victimization became most manifest. The head teacher said that he could not offer her a positive reference, saying that he would not have been willing to extend her appointment at his own school, so how could he mislead another head teacher about his feelings? In his opinion, she had mishandled the incident itself and had failed to cope with her own emotions following it. Sarah asked if this was solely a consequence of her reaction to the violent incident. He denied this but could not offer examples of any flaws in her teaching performance prior to the incident, and indeed he had given her a shining report just prior to the Christmas break. He told her that it was generally felt that she would not be able to adapt to teaching in a rough urban school, and that she might be better in a quiet rural setting with younger pupils. Sarah was totally desolated by this interview and decided to return to university to take a higher degree, leaving teaching for ever.

In this case, the head teacher's evasion of his own responsibility to provide support, the unwillingness of Sarah's colleagues to look for the complex interaction of determinants for the incident, and Sarah's own self-blaming attitude all illustrate the process of victimization.

Victimization is certainly symptomatic of the more general failure to recognize the structural features which precipitate violence. Seeing individuals as responsible fudges essential issues. All of the statistics indicate that in every caring profession there has been an increase in the amount of violent attacks. This cannot be attributed to some sudden decrement in the skills or personal qualities of individual practitioners. The truth of the matter is that the caring professions are being asked to deal with more difficult situations. Teachers are having to handle pupils up to an older age (often against the wishes of young people who would rather leave school) and in an economy where they know very few will find good jobs as a reward for effort at school. Health service personnel are working in a system which is starved of resources and which cannot hope to provide adequate health care. Social workers, probation officers and health visitors are, as a result of changes in mental health and penal legislation, having to take over the care of people in the community who would previously have been cared for in institutions. These changes in the job descriptions of the caring professions go some way toward explaining the perceived increased incidence of violence. The task facing practitioners is really no longer the same as it used to be.

The good news is that the publicity which social scientists have given to processes of victimization over recent years seems to be having an effect. Recent research (Winkel and Denkers, 1995) has shown that blaming the victim is not so evident now as earlier studies suggested. Recognition of the phenomenon will help to contain it.

FAILURE TO REPORT INCIDENTS

The major problem with developing good descriptions of the incidences and forms of violence towards practitioners is that many incidents are unreported by the victim. There are many reasons for this. These include: lack of an organizational policy or guidelines on reportage; ignorance of the policy which exists; poor access to the mechanisms for reporting; and the time and effort required to make a report. However, they also include reasons derived from the processes of victimization: the assumption that being attacked will be treated as a personal failure; the fear that litigation might result; the belief that violence is an integral part of the job. Together these factors are powerful inhibitors of any accurate reportage.

This is one of the most sad side-effects of victimization. It means that practitioners who could be helped never seek support. It also means that the evidence which might be most effective in rebutting the 'blaming' stereotype cannot be accumulated. It means that profiles of assaults are probably biased, perhaps towards those which are more severe, whose effects cannot be hidden, or to those which take place in settings where witnesses are present. This, in turn, means that risk-estimation must continue to be wrong against data which are known to be flawed.

Any measures which improve incident report rates should be welcomed. Better information would aid prevention and post-assault support, and this is clearly a matter for management to address. Proper, user-friendly systems for reporting should be in place, operating in a 'no-blame' culture (discussed further in Chapter 7) so as to encourage accuracy. The information should be collated and analysed in a manner which helps people to improve their own practice, as data collection for its own sake will not generate compliance or accuracy. The major responsibility for improving reportage lies with management, but individuals can contribute a great deal. You can change what happens by ensuring that you do report incidents and that you encourage colleagues to do the same.

FACING VICTIMIZATION

Images which victimize practitioners might be assumed to change to keep abreast of changing reality, but one of the problems with stereotypes is that they are horrifically difficult to change. Evidence which invalidates them is discounted and exceptions can always be made to the rule if an example really cannot be ignored. This particular stereotype needs to be tackled head-on by all members of the caring professions. The first step along the way is for individuals to realize that they have been accepting the stereotype and to reject it. Then another image must be set up in opposition. This might describe practitioner victims as the front line troops in society's battle against bad education, poor health and social deprivation; people who regard their own safety as less important than the need to provide the service; and so on. The task is to generate an image which is positive but realistic. You might like to try to list the types of characteristics such an image should contain and consider what evidence could be marshalled to support it if challenged.

In seeking to rectify the ill-effects of the current stereotype it would be nonsense to ignore the fact that practitioners sometimes **are** responsible for the ignition of an incident. The object is not to paint practitioners crowned with haloes; it may be true that carers are sometimes involved in the physical abuse of their clients, patients or pupils. There are no large-scale statistics on carer–client violence. It is not the sort of information which would be readily recorded since the client rarely has the channels available to voice complaints. But there is sufficient, well-grounded anecdotal information to make the existence of carer–client violence an undeniable reality. There is a great need for independent research to establish the actual magnitude of the problem.

THE ROLE OF THE POPULAR PRESS

Reports of violence are believed to sell newspapers and reports of violence committed against practitioners are all grist to the mill of

the popular press. While a content analysis of the reports of practitioner deaths tends to present the victim in a sympathetic way, survivors tend to get a rougher ride, with the incident typically being
sensationalized. The system of values to which journalists adhere
give priority to novelty and the twist in the tale which will hook the
reader. This means that they will look for the feature of the incident
which is most distinctive, surprising or absurd when reporting an
attack. Frequently, this means focusing upon the reaction of the practitioner, and anything which is incongruous or suspect will be highlighted.

For instance, in the case of a social worker who was held hostage
by a woman with a crossbow, the press focused upon the fact that he
had expressed concern that a message be passed on for his dog to be
looked after. This was over-interpreted as indicating that he did not
consider the threat to be serious and was effectively used to minimize the importance of the crime which the woman had committed.
The social worker felt that he had been ridiculed by the press and
had been made to seem inadequate for being unable to defuse a
minor incident. Yet he had self-consciously used the talk about his
dog as a diversionary tactic. Perhaps the most distressing aspect of
such press representations is that the individual has virtually no
means of redressing the image created.

From a victim's point of view, the pattern of reportage in the press
is likely to reinforce the sub-cultural preconceptions about the char-
acter of assaulted practitioners. The press are in effect merely carica-
turing the stereotype, but, by doing so, they perpetuate and
accentuate it.

There is another issue regarding the media coverage of practitioner assaults which needs to be considered. This concerns the likelihood that media coverage of violence to the caring professions will
stimulate even more people to be aggressive with practitioners. For
some time there has been a debate about the effects of violence por-
trayed by the mass media, and there seems to be some evidence that
watching violence on TV is associated with subsequent violence in
children. However, there is no strong evidence that watching violence on TV causes people to be violent. There is no similar relationship between press coverage of violence and readers' behaviour.
There are, of course, exceptions: the so-called 'copy cat' crimes. But
these are rare. It seems unlikely therefore that press reports of
assaults against carers will incite additional attacks.

However, there may be a more indirect route from press portray-
als to client violence. Members of the caring professions themselves

may be influenced by press reports. Their risk estimates may be affected, their general anxiety level may be changed, their perception of particular types of client group may be altered, and so on. These changes may influence their interactions with clients and become self-fulfilling prophesies of violence. The chain reaction is obviously tenuous but it cannot be dismissed. For instance, teachers seeing the press coverage both of surveys of the profession and of the juicy examples of violence included to give the story 'human interest' are unlikely to ignore the implications for their own classrooms.

SELF-ASSESSMENT

After reading this chapter, you might consider doing a rather different sort of self-assessment exercise. Firstly, find a current report of an assault against a member of your own profession in the press. Analyse the image of the victim and the image of the assailant. What are represented to be their motives, actions and characteristics? To what extent is the report judgmental or evaluative? How far does the image of the victim comply with the dominant stereotype which has been described? Secondly, try to imagine that you are the victim described. How would you react to the coverage? What sort of support would you be looking for from colleagues? The exercise is meant to help you to read the implicit messages in newspaper reports which you receive sometimes without knowing it. It may also help you to erase your own stereotype of practitioner victims. Turn back to the exercise on p.54 and see what your answers would be now.

CHAPTER SUMMARY

❑ Strong stereotypes of practitioners who are the victims of assault exist. They are believed to be: risk-takers, inflexible, demanding, provocative, incompetent, authoritarian and inexperienced.
❑ There is no evidence to suggest that the stereotype is an accurate picture of victims. In fact, victims are very heterogeneous.
❑ Reactions to assault may involve a series of stages: the crisis (up to 90 minutes after the attack); post-crisis depression; medium term effects (involving high anxiety and fear levels); and longer term effects (typified by the symptoms of Post Traumatic Stress Disorder). PTSD symptoms include: persistent re-experiencing of the event in one or more ways (flashbacks, dreams, waking dreams, etc);

avoidance of the stimuli associated with the trauma; continuous increased arousal (manifested in sleeplessness, irritability, problems in thinking and concentrating).

❏ Emotional responses to assault include a predictable sequence which passes from fear, to surprise, to anger and finally to guilt.

❏ Victims differ in their reactions to trauma. The adverse effects are exaggerated if: the victim is already highly stressed; has depressive cognitive styles; lacks a social support network; accepts the negative stereotype of victims; and achieves self-esteem only through work activities.

❏ The assaulted are subject to victimization as a result of biases in attribution (the actor–observer difference and the *Just World Hypothesis*).

❏ Victimization goes some way towards explaining the resistance which exists in most practitioner groups against reporting assaults. Failure to report is also a product of organizations refusing to provide user-friendly, 'no-blame' reporting systems.

Chapter Six

Avoidance, Escape and Control

Consider the following scenarios and decide what you would do in each case.

❏ You have just joined the teaching staff at a school. One of the male pupils, aged 14, is disruptive in the first class you take him for. He ignores your instructions to behave and is being egged on by a small band of other pupils. When you tell him to be quiet, he threatens to 'see to you later'.

❏ You are a social worker whose long-term schizophrenic client has attacked his elderly parents again and you are asked to make an assessment with a psychiatrist with a view to taking the client compulsorily into a psychiatric hospital. Before you get to his house, he disappears but is reported to have gone down the road to a local community centre.

In deciding what to do, what factors would you consider? What additional information would you require before estimating the risk of violence? What assumptions would you make about the person you are dealing with in each case? Having calculated the risk, what would you seek to do to ensure your own safety? How would your strategies for ensuring your safety differ in the two scenarios? Write notes on the factors which you are taking into consideration. It will be useful to compare the answers you give now to the answers you give after reading this chapter.

RECOGNIZE YOUR OWN OBJECTIVES

Before looking at some of the coping strategies available to you, it will be useful to spend a moment analysing the objectives that you have in developing aggression management skills. Obviously, you want to increase your own safety. However, most practitioners will be influenced by three other underlying imperatives.

1. The strategies for coping with violence must be professionally acceptable: they must not abrogate the fundamental values of the caring professions.

2. The strategies should not alienate the clients, patients or pupils in general. Alienating those who are violent may not be seen to be a problem but alienating others who are not dangerous by imposing general rules for practitioner protection may well be seen as a problem.

3. The strategies must be in keeping with the image of their institution that employers of practitioners wish to maintain. This will in turn be affected by the political and economic environment in which employers must operate.

Consequently, choice of strategy is not only dictated by its probable efficiency in any particular situation. In the end, the package of avoidance, escape and control strategies adopted will depend upon the preoccupations of individual practitioners and the priorities of the organizations within which they work. If they are to be effective, virtually all of the strategies require the actions of individual practitioners to be supported by the procedures and policy set by their employer. In this chapter, some of the prime options available to the individual practitioner are described. In the next chapter, the organizational support necessary for coping with aggression will be examined in some detail.

STRATEGIES OF AVOIDANCE

The first lesson to learn in coping with aggression is that it is best avoided altogether – you should avoid situations where violence is likely to happen. This is obviously not always feasible and other strategies will need to be used then, but where avoidance is possible it should be recognized as an *honourable* option.

THE RISK ESTIMATE

You can only avoid aggression if you have enough information about the situation to make an accurate prediction of the behaviour of the people involved. The cues that you should be looking for were summarized in the *Dangerousness Checklist* in Chapter 3. The risk estimate you make will be affected by the biases and stereotyping mentioned in Chapter 3 unless you take pains to correct for them. You should always err on the side of caution in correcting your risk estimates. Ask yourself:

● Am I under-estimating my own vulnerability because the issues involved in this situation are familiar to me?

● Am I allowing my view about this person to be swayed by the fact that they come from a background or are a member of social category (for example, socio-economic class) which I have found non-violent in the past?

● Am I ignoring new information that is coming in as I go along and sticking too rigidly to my initial risk estimate?

● Am I being lulled into an inappropriate sense of security because I have faced this type of situation many times before?

● Am I paying enough attention to the details of this particular situation?

Effectively, this self-interrogation serves to heighten your awareness, pushing you to abandon any simple preconceptions.

AVOIDANCE STRATEGIES

Once you have a risk estimate which indicates aggression is likely, two major avoidance strategies should be considered.

1. **Do not proceed to make contact:** report your estimate of the risk to your line manager or supervisor or senior colleague and come to a joint decision about the appropriate course of action.

2. **Make a preliminary, circumscribed contact:** this can entail contact at a distance, such as using the phone to check details which may influence your estimate of risk, or it may entail rearranging by post the venue or time for the contact so that back-up is available if trouble occurs.

The first option (no contact) should be regarded as the optimal response. Of course, it will only be useful if practitioners operating in senior or middle management roles accept that it is part of their job to develop corporate plans for dealing with a contact that is deemed risky. The response to each high risk contact will need to be individually tailored, but it is also possible and *necessary* for organizations to develop general guidelines and procedures for handling such situations. For some organizations, one particularly attractive possibility is the use of specialists specifically trained to take over high risk contacts.

The second option (contained contact) may not be feasible in some contexts such as in schools or in hospitals. It is mainly viable for practitioners outside institutional contexts, and works best if it is embedded in standard operating procedures. This issue will be considered again in Chapter 7.

STRATEGIES OF DE-ESCALATION AND ESCAPE

Even where estimates of risk indicate that avoidance would be sensible, it is not always possible. For instance, it would be farcical to suggest that a nurse doing night duty in an accident ward could simply ignore the needs of a belligerent but injured drunk even though all of the predictors indicate high risk. The fact that he or she will anticipate trouble, even though it cannot be avoided, is a necessary precursor to self-protection. Making a risk estimation is important even where avoidance is impossible, as it sensitizes you to the need to consider what you would do if any aggression occurs.

Assuming that some practitioners will always need to put themselves at risk in order to do their work, the next set of strategies you need to become familiar with entail skills of de-escalating aggression and escaping the violent situation. Once the aggressive encounter begins there are tactics which can be deployed and individual skills are vital in the use of such tactics. However, organizational support is also important. Many of these tactics will work only if the organization provides the right physical environment, the right information systems, and the right management back up. Unfortunately, few practitioners know how they should behave when facing someone who is about to be violent, and we will now look at this problem.

WHAT DO YOU THINK YOU WOULD DO?

You should take time now to write down a list of the actions that you would take if:

a) you were faced with a youth holding a broken bottle who was hesitating just before striking you;

b) if you encountered a frantic, semi-naked woman standing at the head of the stairs in her home carrying her recently-dead baby in one hand and a kitchen knife in the other.

You will have noticed that you are being asked to list what you would *do*, not what you would *think* or how you would *feel*. The actions listed might include what you would say, where you would try to position yourself, or what physical contact you might try.

One study of social workers showed that most people, when asked how they would respond to threatened violence, eventually said they would try to reason with the assailant or to move away slowly. The truth is, however, that those with experience of an assault knew that when they had been faced with the real situation they had most frequently frozen and failed to do anything. They were too shocked and surprised by the turn of events to be able to propel themselves into action. This is why it is important to think about what you might do.

If you have gone through the *Dangerousness Checklist* regularly and calculated the risk of violence before contact is made, violence will not take you by surprise when it occurs. Mental rehearsal of what alternative strategies are open to you in the face of violence is valuable. Going calmly through your available options many times beforehand will make it easier for you to respond swiftly in the crisis situation. This will minimize the likelihood of personal injury and any escalation of the incident.

WHAT SHOULD YOU DO?

Evidence from many incidents indicates that certain types of action are most likely to de-escalate aggression and allow escape. The following are frequently recommended useful tactics.

• Give the impression of being calm, self-controlled and confident without being dismissive or overbearing.

• Keep talking, using as normal a tone of voice as possible.

• Changing the tone of your voice (for example, raising its pitch or volume) has sometimes been used successfully to attract the attention of an assailant who is manic and whose attention needs to be grabbed before any sensible exchange of information can be achieved.

• Mood-matching has sometimes proved useful: the assailant who shouts is shouted back at; calm intensity is greeted with equal intensity. This seems to work, if it works at all, by encouraging assailants to realize what they are doing because they see what you are doing.

• Try diversionary tactics, such as offering to make tea, claiming to be worried about something outside, saying you are hungry, making a joke, anything which takes the assailant's attention from the trigger or incitement for violence.

• If the attack is designed to establish the assailant's dominance (as may happen in sexual assaults), feign submission, using talk to redirect attention.

• As soon as the risk of attack is evident, check on the availability of escape routes or exits and work your way towards them. Try to put some large object between yourself and the assailant or manoeuvre yourself so that you are not trapped in a corner. Never turn your back on an assailant. If you try to escape, leave moving gradually backwards.

• Do not approach an armed assailant – maintain your distance.

• An armed assailant should be explicitly asked to put the weapon down. You should try to take the initiative where possible in telling the assailant what you want him or her to do. Slow repetition of instructions may be necessary.

• Remove potential weapons where possible.

• Try to disperse any onlookers who may be acting to incite the assailant. It is worth noting that it may be naïve to expect any assistance from onlookers, even when they have no affiliation with the assailant. Bystander apathy is a well-established phenomenon: when people are in a crowd or group, especially in contexts where they are anonymous and unsure of their responsibility, they will not step in to provide help to someone else. You can break such bystander apathy by making a highly specific request for assistance from a particular person in the crowd. The trick is to identify someone and give them precise instructions about what they should do.

It is often suggested that you should also use nonverbal channels to calm the situation. This is not so easy to do in practice as it may sound in principle, and the advice given differs. Some people claim that you should maintain eye contact with the assailant; others say this can be interpreted as aggressive and should be avoided. Some claim sudden movements will arouse retaliations; others claim stillness will incite an onslaught. In reality, it is impossible to make generalizations about the role of nonverbal communication in such contexts. Much will depend upon the prior pattern of interactions with the assailant and the reason for the attack. The vital thing is that practitioners should be aware that this form of communication may be operating during the attack. Where a violent incident lasts longer than a few minutes (and some have been known to last for hours) it may be possible to judge which patterns of non-verbal responses are most effective.

IMPLICATIONS OF THE ASSAULT CYCLE IN CHOOSING TACTICS

During the trigger phase, the potential assailant is most likely to be anxious and suspicious. Your focus should be upon reducing the level of arousal and making yourself non-threatening (giving the appearance of empathy, genuineness, patience, concern, and so on). You can reinforce the fact that you are concerned by:

● reminding the person that you have offered help in the past;
● paraphrasing and restating what the person is saying to you, thus proving that you are listening and that you understand;
● offering evidence that you understand how the person feels by naming the emotion, for example, 'You must be feeling...';
● using open questions to encourage the person to talk and thus to reflect upon the situation;
● offering diversions such as asking whether they have seen some friend or family member recently, asking if they need the toilet, offering a cigarette.

Tactics to avoid include: direct, confrontational questions about the cause of their aggressiveness; direct threats; invasion of the person's personal space; judgmental or critical statements.

If you enter the escalation phase, it becomes obvious that the calming tactics suggested are not working. This is the time to shift quite definitely to tactics designed to manage your own risk levels. These will include calling for back up from colleagues; executing a tactical withdrawal from the situation; clearing away potential weapons; explaining the consequences for the assailant of any further aggression and being specific in what you would like him or her to do to end the incident. During escalation, it is sometimes possible to negotiate a compromise that leads to cessation of the attack. For instance, you can offer concessions if some aspect of the aggressive behaviour is curtailed. So, you might say, 'If you put the knife down, I will telephone your GP/your wife/the manager'. You can also push for small concessions which give you purchase to push harder for big ones. For example, if you feel trapped in a room, you might ask your captor to let you open a window or turn on the lights as a precursor to asking them to open the door. It has been shown that assailants who accede to small requests are subsequently more likely to agree to large concessions. The initial concessions seem to predispose them to greater positivity.

If de-escalation fails, the crisis phase will offer little opportunity for constructive control of the situation. Remember, you should try not to freeze: shout, run, use an alarm – do something. By this point, your objective should be to either physically restrain the assailant as the attack is launched or stop the attack using 'breakaway' tactics. Breakaway tactics cannot be effectively conveyed in written descriptions. They involve simplified versions of martial art holds to disarm or temporarily throw the assailant. They are not simple to learn or use, and if you are interested in learning about them it is important to get thorough training.

If you handle the crisis phase without injury, you will still probably have to face the recovery phase. Alternatively, you might find yourself pulled in to deal with the assailant in the recovery phase after the initial assault has taken place on someone else. This is a most dangerous time. You must allow time for the arousal level to subside, and you should not shift into analysing the incident or demanding explanations from the assailant at this point. Any attempt to analyse the problem at this stage could easily result in a sudden return to violence. In this 30–90 minute phase, you are most valuable if you make clear that there will be a return to 'normality': maximize the evident staff control of the situation; give clear instructions about what you expect the assailant to do; and prepare the assailant for the likely impact of the post-crisis depression phase.

The post-crisis depression phase is not absolutely inevitable. For some assailants, the violence leaves no trace of guilt, shame, remorse or sadness. For most there is some element of these emotions. There is also a realization that the problems which triggered the outburst are still there, unaffected by it. At this point, the practitioner with appropriate skills will be engaged in counselling and problem-solving (offering advice, information, and assistance for the assailant in analysing the origins of the difficulties).

If you were the practitioner who was assaulted, it is unlikely that you would be the best person to cope with the assailant in either the

SELF-ASSESSMENT EXERCISE 6:
WHAT DID HE DO WRONG?

This is the case of a GP, James, who was badly injured during an assault in a patient's home. Work through the case history and identify each time James did or said something which put him more at risk. The notes at the end of the case history indicate the main things he did wrong (errors of commission or omission). You may be able to spot other things. You should also consider what he should have done instead. What alternative actions were possible?

James, 43, had been acting as a locum in a GP practice for three days when he was called out at 2 a.m. to attend a sick child. He took the telephone call himself, ascertained that the woman calling was the mother of the child, that the child was having difficulties breathing and that the mother was distraught. He left immediately. No one else was aware of the call and he left no record of where he was going. He did not look at the family's medical records before setting off. He had some difficulty finding the house because he was new to the area and was very concerned that his delay might endanger the child.

James rushed from his car to the front door, forgetting to lock the car which had some medical instruments and drugs in the boot. The front door of the house was wide open. He heard shouting from inside, a man and woman obviously involved in a fight. The woman was accusing the man of hitting her baby. She screamed that he had killed the child. James went straight towards the sound of the fight. As he got to the room they were in, he saw a female child of about four years of age prone on the sofa, apparently unconscious. James said in an angry tone, 'What have you been doing? Both of you shut up. This child is in a serious condition'. He went over to the child and began to examine her. At this point, the man, who was clearly drunk, pushed aside the mother and advanced on James, telling him to get his hands off the girl – she was his daughter and he knew what was best for her. James ignored the man. The man shouted, 'If you don't keep off, I'll smash you'. James said nothing and remained with his back to the man, trying to resuscitate the little girl. The man grabbed James from behind, saying, 'You're all the same. No respect'. James fell backwards, recovered himself and started to push the man away. The man tried to cradle the child in his arms. James mumbled, 'You will hurt her, you fool', and tried to pull the man away. The man turned and punched James several times in the face and stomach.

--- *continued*

continued --

For several minutes, James was unconscious. He awoke to find himself locked in a small dark understairs cupboard. Outside he could hear what sounded like a struggle between the man and woman. Furniture was being broken and the woman was shouting abuse as she threw things at the man. After about ten minutes, the man shouted 'That's it!' and James heard a door slam. There was then complete silence for a long time. James tried to break down the door of the cupboard but it was firm. It was about one hour later when the police arrived and discovered him. A neighbour had phoned them after she was awakened by the man breaking all the windows on James' car. The mother had been knocked out and was still unconscious when the police arrived. The police told James that the family had a long history of domestic violence; the man was suspected of abusing the child and the woman had only recently returned to the house from a refuge for battered wives. The child was taken to hospital and was found to be suffering from several cracked ribs and concussion.

WHERE DID JAMES GO WRONG?

● He should have left some message as to where he was going. He was going to a family he had never seen before, in the middle of the night, when he knew the mother was distraught. If the neighbour had not rung the police, he could have been in the cupboard a long time.

● He should have considered calling the ambulance service to help him deal with the child. If the breathing difficulties were grave, he would have wasted valuable time before calling them. However, the fact that he did not call them is unsurprising, since he would have been aware that they were likely to get to the scene later than he did, given the shortage of ambulances available.

● He did not examine the medical records of the family. He had them available by modem link to the practice's computerized records. If he had done so, he would have seen a caution concerning a previous assault by the man, who was the child's step-father. Of course, often locums in the middle of the night will not have access to medical records. They are unlikely to have had any past dealings with the patient and this means that they are inevitably disadvantaged in making risk assessments.

● He did not lock his car. The risk of GPs being mugged for

-- *continued*

continued _____

drugs which they carry are high, as are the risks of their cars being targeted for theft. He should have ensured himself against theft as far as possible. There is always the possibility that the emergency call was a set-up just to rob him.

● He did not call for backup as soon as he heard the sound of the fight.

● He did not say who he was. Nor did he try to calm the man or woman down. He may have been right to be primarily concerned with the child's health, but in doing so he placed himself at great risk and this could have been avoided by making use of a less incendiary set of opening remarks.

● He ignored the man's approach and ignored his threat. In such a situation it is foolish to ignore the threat. He was too focused on his medical duty to the child.

● He should not have tried to pull the man away from the child. He should not have called him a fool (especially after the man had already indicated that he thought that other people showed him no respect).

● He did not try to call for help after he heard the man leave the house. It is most likely that he would have been reacting to the shock of the situation by that point, resulting in a form of freezing – a lack of constructive action.

Throughout this incident, James pursued the priority of dealing with the child. This was laudable, but his failure to handle the potential and actual violence meant that, in the end, he was unable to help the child properly. Sometimes practitioners can only satisfy their main duty of care by first ensuring their own safety.

It is sometimes useful as a training exercise to go through reports of incidents and identify what should have been done differently. Obviously, 20:20 vision is possible in hindsight, but the process of identifying faults in the performance of other people will sensitize you to problems in your own practice.

recovery or post-crisis depression phases as you would be going through the same phased response yourself. It is worth remembering this. Too often practitioners try to re-establish the relationship with the assailant too quickly – especially if the attack has been handled effectively in the crisis or escalation phases.

ANXIETY MANAGEMENT

All of the strategies recommended rely upon the practitioner involved being able to remain reasonably calm. They would be impossible for anyone who was unable to manage their own anxiety. Anxiety management techniques are primarily based upon knowing how you personally respond to stress. They are founded upon first acquiring an understanding of what physiological and psychological consequences stress produces and then upon having a battery of tactics for ameliorating their effects. Training for handling aggression should include methods of anxiety management.

One of the key factors in reducing the anxiety response in violent situations is the mental rehearsal of coping strategies prior to the event. Just considering the risk and the possibilities introduces a mental hardiness which is invaluable. This is really a variant of the more traditional methods of anxiety management which involve 'desensitizing' unpleasant objects or events by associating them with deep relaxation and an enhanced sense of personal control.

Two other techniques are usually used in anxiety management. The first involves learning to relax muscular tension at will. This merely takes much practice when outside an anxiety-arousing situation and can then be used in such situations to reduce the physiological response to threat. The second entails 'positive guided imagery', which basically means thinking about nicer things and better times in the face of adversity. This technique may not be practicable in the face of violence but it may be something to be considered after the event to restore wellbeing.

As long as anxiety can be held at bay when facing violence, it is possible in any extended incident to use standard counselling skills in addition to the approaches described above. This might mean that basic training for some practitioner groups would have to be extended to encompass counselling skills. Such skills would include knowing how to use assertiveness appropriately; that is, knowing how to acknowledge other people's feelings and rights and still resist them.

Survivors of violent assaults have attested to the usefulness of the strategies recommended. For instance, one social worker who was tied up by a woman and threatened with a crossbow (see also p.67) reported later that there were four aspects of his behaviour during the assault which in retrospect he felt to have been correct:

1. He had been assertive and had acknowledged the demand she was making (wanting him to write to the housing office to seek a transfer for her) which triggered the incident, but refused to comply with the demand.

2. He had challenged her and called her bluff when she first produced the crossbow, calmly telling her to put it away.

3. He had used diversionary tactics (claiming he was a vegetarian and would be difficult to hold hostage because she would not be able to feed him; trying to get her to pass on a message to get his dog fed).

4. He had controlled his anxiety by holding on to the thought that the incident would eventually end safely.

Another example comes from a health visitor who went to visit a woman suffering from depression whose child had eczema. She arrived at the house to find the husband wielding an axe. The health visitor had no information on the family since they were new to the area and had been a self-referral. Faced with the axe, she tried diversionary tactics. Noticing that there were voodoo artefacts in the room, she began to talk about the man's voodoo practices. She was ultimately allowed to leave once the conversation finished.

STRATEGIES OF PHYSICAL CONTROL

PHYSICAL RESTRAINT

One way to control violence is to use force, and in the crisis phase it may be the only option left. The legal position is that the carer should use minimum reasonable force (that is, enough to stop the aggressor and protect yourself but no more). The definition of 'reasonable' is not what the victim of the assault might have felt was reasonable in the heat of the moment during the attack, but what they would have thought reasonable if they had time for reflection. The level of force thought reasonable will vary with circumstances, depending upon the characteristics of the assailant, the degree of force being used and the possibility of dealing with the attack in other ways. The general assumption is that the force should focus on restraint being used to overpower the attacker rather than to injure. If the assailant is armed and attempting to inflict significant harm, then a degree of force sufficient to stop the attack, which may include rendering the assailant unconscious or inflicting serious harm, will possibly be considered justified. Under no circumstances should more force than is absolutely necessary be used. There is no place for the macho syndrome which calls for force to be met with force, irrespective of circumstance.

Common guidelines for physical restraint recommend that the person is held near a major joint to avoid dislocation and not near the throat, neck, chest, abdomen or fingers. You should avoid interfering with breathing, blood supply, or sexual areas. If immobilization is necessary, hold the assailant front down on a soft surface and apply pressure to the upper back, and then the trunk and legs if necessary. Especially with elderly assailants, it is advised that they should be held by clothing if possible to avoid bruising and fractures.

Despite these commonly accepted guidelines, there have been growing numbers of fatalities at the hands of practitioners attempting to use physical restraint. The dangers are enormous. Before using physical restraint techniques you must be aware of how easy it is to seriously injure someone with them. Controlled physical restraint is often only feasible if it is possible to call upon assistance. This should be assistance from another practitioner – practitioners are usually advised against involving other clients in the restraint of an assailant as the legal implications of their involvement are complex.

Restraint needs to be followed up with removal from the scene of the violence and isolation is typically used. If you anticipate using physical restraint, it is a good idea to know where you intend to isolate the assailant and to ensure that the place is stripped of hazardous implements. If it is anticipated that physical restraint will be necessary, it may be as well to involve the police at the earliest opportunity. Police can enter dwellings to prevent a breach of the peace, so anyone who reckons that the risks are great can arrange to have an officer by their side.

TIME-OUTS

In institutional contexts, the problem of control of violence can be tackled in a different way. Where the violence is minor, a convention of imposing 'time-outs' can be implemented. The person who is showing signs of aggression is asked to go to a room set aside for the purpose, stays there alone for a short time and then returns. Time-outs are designed to allow arousal levels to drop naturally and thus de-escalate the situation.

BEHAVIOUR MODIFICATION REGIMES

Time-outs are sometimes supplemented by the use of more explicit 'extinction' regimes. These rely upon negatively reinforcing (that is, punishing or failing to reward, for instance by withdrawing privileges) unwanted aggression. As a means of controlling violence in practice, these methods are only viable in contexts where the practitioner has control over the things which the person finds rewarding or punishing for some lengthy period. They can also only be pursued after a full analysis of the functions which the violent behaviour serves. It is only by understanding what the violence is aimed at achieving that it is possible to shape a schedule of rewards or punishments which can eradicate it. Functional analyses are also rather difficult in the short term or outside of an institutional setting. If behaviour modification techniques are used it is worth noting that the reinforcement regime should be routinized so that there is no opportunity for intermittent (and consequently very powerful) reinforcement of violent acts. It is also worth bearing in mind that after the violent acts are curtailed by behaviour modification, there may be what is called a 'post-extinction burst' of violent activity. This is something like a final fling. It should be anticipated and its effects minimized, possibly through the containment of the individual during the risk period.

SOCIETAL ATTITUDES

All these forms of violence control are centred upon intervention at the level of the specific individual. Many of the caring professions are now arguing that there should be an attempt at the social control of violence towards practitioners. This would entail campaigns to change attitudes about what is acceptable behaviour in relation to the caring professions. The idea is that the mass media could lead people to view carers and their professional roles in a different light. The problem with such a plan is that even if attitudes could be changed, there is no assurance that behaviour would follow suit.

A FRAMEWORK FOR DEVELOPING COPING STRATEGIES

Think again about the two scenarios at the start of this chapter. Review the considerations which you listed when you first thought about them. Has your approach changed? If so, how? If this chapter has had the desired effect, you will now be working through a series of stages when considering these scenarios.

Stage 1: Estimate the Risk – you will examine the situation for the cues to risk summarized in the *Dangerousness Checklist;*

Stage 2: Check for Risk Estimation Biases – review whether you are being unduly affected by the biases known to affect risk calculations (availability, anchoring, representativeness and subjective immunity effects) or by your own stereotypes;

Stage 3: Identify Strategies – consider whether it is necessary to face the risk at all *(avoidance option).* If not, you will mentally rehearse the sorts of things you would need to do and say to de-escalate aggression or to escape if it cannot be quelled *(escape option).* You will have assessed the viability and ethics of using physical restraint should the need arises *(control option).*

Stage 4: Ready Yourself – try to manage your anxiety so that you can optimize your ability to think clearly and quickly. You will recognize the anticipatory changes in your own physiological state and be able to interpret them sensibly.

The central argument in this chapter has been that you should use all available predictors of violence to estimate the risks that you face, even though the predictors will indicate some contacts as dangerous which later prove to be perfectly safe. It is better to be sensitized to contacts which prove safe, than to fail to pin-point ones which prove hazardous. Before going into a risky situation, strategies for handling violence should be rehearsed. Dogmatic statements about what should be done in any specific situation are pointless. The individual involved must be ready to analyse all available information and choose his or her strategies, a choice which will be heavily influenced by self-knowledge. Such tactical decisions can only be made properly if the individual can remain calm. Familiarity with anxiety management techniques could be productively harnessed in such situations. Escape should be the prime objective in most cases. Attempts to control violence should be limited to restraint or the use of programmes designed to systematically discourage aggression.

CHAPTER SUMMARY

❑ The strategies you use in coping with aggression must be professionally acceptable, minimally alienating to the people you care for, and in keeping with the policy guidelines and expectations of your employer.

❑ Avoidance of situations and encounters likely to entail aggression is an honourable option. This can only be achieved if you are willing to make every effort to calculate potential risks accurately.

❑ Dangerous situations sometimes cannot be avoided. In this case, you should know how to use strategies of de-escalation and escape. A range of tactics can be used to de-escalate aggression. These include: maintaining you own self-control; continuing talking normally; mood-matching; diversion of the assailant's attention; feigned submission; using furniture layout to provide some protection; maintaining your distance from the assailant; making specific requests for changes in the assailant's behaviour; dispersing onlookers who might incite further aggression; and seeking help from bystanders.

❑ Choice of tactic should be related to the Assault Cycle. The tactics that work best in the Trigger Phase focus upon illustrating that you understand and acknowledge how the assailant is feeling and attempt to diminish the confrontation. The tactics that work in the Escalation Phase centre upon evacuation from the situation, removal of likely weapons, or negotiation of a cessation of the aggression. The Crisis Phase is not amenable to the use of tactics other than physical restraint or breakaway techniques, and it is important not to freeze in this phase. The Recovery Phase is very dangerous. The best tactic is to allow time to pass so that arousal levels subside. The Post-Crisis Depression Phase does not always happen but if it does it requires a shift to counselling and problem-solving approaches. This final phase may be best pursued by someone other than the assaulted practitioner.

❑ Anxiety management techniques are useful. Mental rehearsal of tactics prior to entering a violent situation can lower anxiety levels during the incident itself.

❑ There are a number of ethical and legal issues surrounding the use of physical restraint in response to violence which need to be considered. The practitioner must use minimum reasonable force.

❑ It is useful to develop a framework for your approach to dealing with aggression. This should involve: estimating the risk; checking for biases in your risk estimates; identifying and mentally rehearsing tactics to be used; and, readying yourself physically and psychologically for the assault.

Chapter Seven

Safety Culture

WHAT IS SAFETY CULTURE?

Over time, every employing organization will develop its own culture. While formal definitions of the concept 'culture' differ in detail, they do converge on central components. Culture comprises the shared attitudes, values and beliefs and encompasses the behavioural norms and expectations which characterize members of a particular group or social category. Ethnologists and anthropologists claim that culture includes everything learned or otherwise acquired by a society that is preserved and passed on to future members. Accordingly, culture acts as an unspoken language to which we react as if in response to some secret complex code never written down but understood by all. Once a culture is established it transcends the individual members of the group.

Organizational cultures often include both explicit and implicit codes about the type of people who should be employed, the way things are to be done and said, the relationship between management and their staff, the importance of satisfying client needs or demands, the significance of the physical working environment, and the factors which motivate productivity, such as material rewards or social recognition.

The organizational cultures of the caring professions are particularly complex. They arise out of a complicated amalgam of professional ethics and codes of practice interacting with the ethos of management systems often imposed by political policy at the local or national level. They are also greatly affected by the traditions and memories of the particular profession. While all members of one class of caring organization might evidence some similarity in their organizational cultures, they will also have idiosyncrasies. For instance, in hospitals the organizational culture emerges from the dynamic exchanges between a host of different care providers (such as doctors, nurses, physiotherapists, nutritionists, ambulance drivers) in the context of management structures which are concerned with financial efficiency. At some level, all hospitals may share features of a common organizational culture but in practice they all possess some unique qualities. The same applies to schools or to social work agencies.

Safety culture is one aspect of organizational culture (Cox and Cox, 1991), and is the product of the individual and group values, attitudes, perceptions, competences, and patterns of behaviour that determine the commitment to, and the style and proficiency of, an organization's health and safety management. It may, in part, be embedded in formal, explicit rules and regulations or procedures and practices. Other aspects of the safety culture will be unwritten, invisible to the uninitiated observer, but understood by most, if not all, of the organization's employees. These covert safety codes are vital determiners of behaviour in many crisis situations. They often determine compliance with, and interpretation of, the manifest safety codes. For example, the formal practice guidelines might state that you should call for assistance if a client with a history of violence threatens you verbally but, if the covert safety code says that that would indicate incompetence or cowardice, there will be great pressure on you to ignore the explicit rules.

In developing strategies for coping with aggression, the caring professions need to consider their safety cultures. As an individual you need to be aware of the safety culture in which you work. Try to complete self-assessment exercise 7 now, before reading the next section on the indicators of safety culture.

INDICATORS OF SAFETY CULTURE

Organizations with a positive safety culture are characterized by communications between members founded upon mutual trust, by shared perceptions of the importance of safety and by consensual confidence in the efficacy of preventive measures which are in operation. There are a series of factors to consider in assessing the safety culture of an organization, falling under the headings: *general organizational factors* and *safety-related organizational factors*.

SELF-ASSESSMENT EXERCISE 7:
YOUR SAFETY CULTURE

Answer 'Yes' or 'No' to the following questions:

● Is it acknowledged by your managers that you are at risk of violent attack while you are at work?
● Is it clear to you what procedures you should follow if you think that you are about to be faced with a potentially violent situation?
● Is it clear to you what to do if you have experienced a violent incident which did not lead to you actually being hurt?
● Do you know what to do if you are assaulted?
● Would you follow the reporting procedures as far as you are aware of them if you were attacked?
● Does responsibility for setting safety policy lie in the hands of identified people?
● Do you think managers are aware of the risks you face?
● Are managers willing to take account of the risks you face?
● Does conflict between individuals result in inadequate information flow to you?
● Are there ways for doing the job which most people use which cut corners on safety precautions in order to get the work done?
● Does management condone deviations from normal operating practices as long as the work gets done?
● Are the skills or abilities of some of your co-workers considered to be better than they actually are and need to be?
● Is compliance with safety regulations superficial?
● Are external experts ignored when they offer advice on safety?
● Are minor incidences of aggression ignored?
● Is provision of training on violence limited to a small proportion of the staff?
● Are individuals who have been assaulted expected to deal with their reactions on their own?
● Are managers defensive with respect to criticism or suggestions about their role in managing violence?

Score one point for every 'Yes' answer you gave on questions 1–8. Score one point for every 'No' answer you gave on questions 9–18. A high score indicates a good safety culture. Anything less than nine should leave you asking whether something can be done to bring about change.

GENERAL ORGANIZATIONAL FACTORS

● Effective communication. Has the organization evidence to demonstrate that all personnel have been informed about, understand and accept corporate goals and the goals of their specific team or sub-group? Is it policy to ensure that people understand and accept the means which must be used to achieve these goals? Are techniques used to ensure that individuals' perceptions of risks and preventative measures are considered by management?

● Good organizational learning. Has the organization proof that its work practices are under continuous review to ensure timely responses to changes in the internal and external environment?

● Self-assessment. Does the organization systematically encourage reflection on operational control and decision-making processes?

● Leadership. Has the organization evidence to show that managers and supervisors have been trained in leadership skills which entail *democratic*, not authoritarian, styles?

● Management of stress. Has the organization adopted schemes to identify managers, supervisors and other personnel who may be subject to life-event stressors which might affect their performance? Are procedures in place for containing the personal and organizational effects of stress symptoms?

Positive answers to these types of questions indicate an organization more likely to have a good safety culture. It is notable that positive safety regimes are found to be associated with egalitarian, open management styles. Authoritarianism, based on minimizing individual responsibility, tends to erode commitment to safety.

SAFETY-RELATED ORGANIZATIONAL FACTORS

There are additional organizational factors specifically related to safety codes which should be considered when assessing safety culture.

● Organizational focus. Is safety management clearly a line management responsibility? Is it an integral part of the line manager's job description? Is safety everyone's problem and responsibility?

● Senior management commitment. Are safety policy and guidelines set by senior management? Do the senior management want to know the details of safety issues and problems? Is paying attention to safety issues given prominent status and reward?

● Management style. Do managers take an interest in the personal, as well as the work, problems of subordinates?

• Management visibility. Has the organization evidence to demonstrate that managers at all levels spend time in the places where their staff do the majority of the work? Do they have a clear understanding of the job on the ground? Do they make a point of discussing safety issues with staff? Is it generally expected that they will do so?

• Two-way communication. Do managers listen and act upon information about safety issues coming from their staff as well as disseminating management policy on safety widely and in a comprehensible fashion?

• Productivity pressures. Has the organization taken explicit steps to detect and eradicate instances where managers allow the need to maximize productivity (for example, increasing caseloads, reducing staffing levels, or cutting material resource support) to influence safety precautions?

• Training. Has the organization adopted a safety training policy? Is this evaluated and updated regularly? Is the practice effect of training assessed?

• Workforce composition. Is the skill level of the workforce adequate for the task-demands? Are experienced and less-experienced staff balanced in numbers and in areas of responsibility and roles?

• Assessment of risk mis-estimation. Does the organization check that staff are able to correctly estimate the risks involved in their work?

• Appropriate employee attitudes to risk. Does the organization monitor employee attitudes to risk-taking? Does it intervene if there is evidence that peer pressure is inciting risk-taking?

Of course, in addition to these organizational factors, you may want to look into the attitudes, values, beliefs and behaviour of individual members of staff when assessing a safety culture. The general argument for focusing upon organizational indicators is based on the assumption that the thoughts, feelings and actions of individuals will be shaped by them. If your concern is to achieve a positive safety culture, you should concentrate your interventions at the level of organizational practices. Change at the individual level will flow from organizational change.

MANAGEMENT ROLE IN COPING WITH AGGRESSION

Exploration of the nature of safety cultures serves to emphasize the role of organizational structure, policy and practice in coping with aggression. Earlier chapters have considered what the individual can do to handle violence; this chapter examines what the organization can do to support the individual in avoidance, escape and control, and, if need be, in surviving the effects of aggressive incidents.

In general, the key elements in the process of managing safety are schematized in Figure 2.

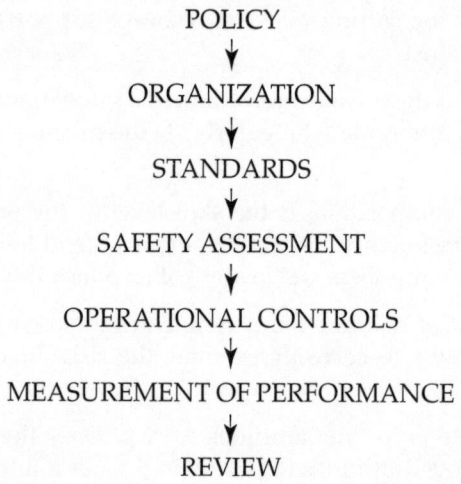

POLICY
↓
ORGANIZATION
↓
STANDARDS
↓
SAFETY ASSESSMENT
↓
OPERATIONAL CONTROLS
↓
MEASUREMENT OF PERFORMANCE
↓
REVIEW

Figure 2: THE PROCESS OF MANAGING SAFETY*

*Note: Each of the seven elements in this process is part of a series of feedback loops as well as being part of the linear process indicated.

To actively manage the safety of staff, an organization must establish its safety policy. The policy may be to establish a good safety culture. At a more mundane level it is most likely to entail objectives with regard to staff safety, tied to a timetable. For instance, the policy might be to reduce by 50 per cent incidents which result in physical harm, over a period of one year.

The organization phase will include, for instance, establishing job descriptions so that individuals at all levels understand their responsibilities with relation to hazardous situations and it may include provision for re-training or instituting new selection criteria for recruitment. It may also include changes in the physical working environment. The organization phase would certainly encompass setting up methods for communicating about safety issues and establishing co-operation on safety promotion.

Setting safety standards will involve the formulation of clear behavioural expectations concerning the response to all aspects of violent incidents (for those immediately involved and for their line managers). They will include requirements about the treatment of clients, patients, and so on. Most importantly, they will specify what is permissible in terms of practitioner aggression and identify limitations to the use of physical control.

Safety assessment will entail a formal evaluation of the organization and standards which have been created. They should be tested in hypothetical scenarios or through book exercises to see whether they are likely to offer the changes in levels of security required. It is at this stage that false assumptions should be identified and the non-obvious disadvantages or weaknesses spotted – some systems sound good in principle but could never work in practice. For instance, a system which always requires the presence of a colleague in any hazardous situation is unlikely to gain acceptance because of the financial implications.

Once a system has passed the formal evaluation, it must be put into practice. This will mean translating it into operational controls: staffing rotas; line manager supervisions; recording and investigation procedures; quality assurance routines; emergency arrangements; training of staff; and so on. Performance within the new system should be measured. Changes in incident rates and in levels of injury should be monitored. Continuous measurement of performance is important but it is no substitute for regular periodic reviews of the impact of the policy and the way it is being implemented. All control systems tend to deteriorate over time as a result of either internal or external changes; hence, learning from experience through the use of audits and performance reviews enables organizations to maintain high standards.

This type of management of safety is now required of all employers with more than five employees throughout Europe. Employers are legally obliged to assess the risks to the health and safety of their employees, and to anyone else who may be affected by their work activity; to record these risks and to take steps to control the risk, establishing emergency procedures where necessary, and ensuring that employees have adequate training to make them capable enough in their jobs so that they can avoid risks.

ORGANIZATIONAL STRATEGIES

As part of their developing safety culture, it is clear that the safety policy that organizations employing carers must create will include a number of facets:

- guidelines for practice;
- training programmes;
- modifications in the working environment;
- post-trauma support for staff;
- management of practitioner violence;
- inter-agency co-operation.

GUIDELINES FOR PRACTICE

Of course, the actual guidelines for practice which have evolved in the light of concern about violence differ across professions because of the nature of their work and the context in which it is done. Establishing guidelines and communicating them to all staff is what matters. The details of their content will depend on the specific context in which you operate. These guidelines would at least be likely to encompass:

- recommendations about the procedure practitioners should follow when they have estimated that the risk of violence is high (this may include the speed with which supervisors or seniors should be alerted, how they should be alerted and who is responsible for alerting them);

- recommendations about the type and extent of back-up necessary for a member of staff making a high risk contact (this may include details of the experience necessary in any additional staff to be called into the situation);

- directions for the ways in which case histories should be reviewed regularly – including the regular review of long-term clients or patients;

- proposals for the way in which a violent client, pupil or patient should be handled immediately after the incident and in the longer term;

• guidance about the involvement of the police. Many agencies are now accepting that violence should result in the involvement of the police and prosecution. Where the offence is not serious enough to merit this, guidance is necessary about how to prevent further minor incidents and about whether and how the victim is to re-establish effective relations with the assailant;

• whatever the sanctions to be used against assailants, where possible potential assailants should be fully aware of their existence (with a view to dissuading them);

• recommendations about how any other clients/pupils/patients present at the time of the assault should be controlled or subsequently counselled. The effects of a violent act upon others present, who may have no immediate part in it, can be considerable. Practitioners need to be briefed on how to manage them. This will differ considerably across professional contexts;

• instructions for the way staff movements can be logged and monitored;

• recommendations for a system which would enable complaints by clients to be investigated and malpractice to be examined. There must be some way of routinely getting the assailant's versions of an incident. There must also be some consistent way of identifying practitioner violence or aggression;

• proposals for a system which will facilitate immediate reporting of violent incidents and provide an adequate and easily accessible data base for liaison with other agencies such as the police, and for the staff themselves.

These sorts of guidelines seem obvious. Yet all too often they are not developed, or if developed, not implemented or policed. Time and again, when fatalities and serious injuries occur and investigations are conducted, basic guidelines have either not been available to the practitioner concerned or have been irrelevant for their situation. Guidelines for practice more often than not become irrelevant because the functions served by the organization have changed and no allowance has been made in the guidelines. For instance, a hostel may start life servicing homeless youths but evolve into a refuge for the serious psychiatric cases who are no longer contained in hospital but reliant upon community care. The practice guidelines in use may not change in keeping with the changing clientele and their very different demands, and such slippage of function can also cause difficulties when it comes to staffing. Staff selection strategies that worked when choosing appropriate people to deal with young homeless may not be effective in picking people to deal with paranoid schizophrenics. The trouble is that new appointments may not reflect the changing demands of the situation. Organizations which have strong safety cultures are unlikely to fail to recognize changes of function or to fail to take them into account in evolving practice guidelines. They will be following the stages in the management of safety outlined in Figure 2 which emphasize the importance of monitoring and reviewing the effectiveness of any measures which are taken. The real problems arise with caring agencies that are amateurish in their approach to safety assessment or measuring performance. These will put their staff most at risk.

TRAINING PROGRAMMES

Organizations must determine what safety training is needed and they have an obligation to provide it. Training should cover:

- competence in assessing risk, including knowledge of the prevalence and indicators of violence which allow realistic risk estimation;
- skills for de-escalating aggression, including negotiation tactics;
- techniques of physical restraint;
- anxiety management methods;
- organizational policy and procedures.

The route to training need not be conventional. One scheme which has been suggested involves lateral transfers between staff of certain grades. Effectively, people at similar levels swap jobs for varying periods of time after briefing each other in the complexities of their work. This allows some to get a respite from continual hard decisions and gives all the opportunity for the exchange of knowledge. Role-play techniques are also highly favoured. One technique involves establishing a series of scenarios dealing with a specific problem, and an actor acts the role of the client in a setting appropriate to the case which is outlined to the practitioner. The role play includes a debriefing with the actor still in role. The interchange can be videotaped and analysed later by a group of practitioners and a facilitator. Such techniques could be incorporated into the training of all professional carers. They provide an immediacy and relevance to the training experience which traditional information dissemination does not offer.

Training should not only include developing skills in predicting and avoiding or controlling violence, but it should also educate the practitioner in the reactions to expect after an assault – the personal emotional response and the reaction of others. There are an increasing number of training packs which can be used for this purpose.

In developing training strategies, it may be useful to highlight the advantages of joint training schemes which take in people from different professional groups. The overwhelming impression gained when the features of attacks and the techniques for avoidance and control are examined is that there are great commonalties across professional groups. With shrinking budgets for training in education, health and social services, it makes economic sense to look for joint training events. It also makes practical sense. Members of these different services frequently have to work together, especially in handling people who are likely to be violent. Subsequent liaison in practice could be facilitated if at least some training were done in common. Such inter-service training should sometimes involve the police force since many strategies for containing violence or dealing with its aftermath entail their involvement.

MODIFICATIONS IN THE WORKING ENVIRONMENT

The most popular recommendations concerning protection by changing the working environment (Brown *et al.*, 1986; Owens and Ashcroft, 1985; Crane, 1986) are:

● make alarm systems available – either personal alarms or room alarms;

● use video systems to monitor isolated areas, or communal areas where staff work alone, so that any assault will be visible to other staff;

● design reception areas so that there is no easy access for clients to staff;

● design room lay-out and choose furniture so as to minimize risks of being trapped or harmed;

● minimize delays and tell people why they have to wait if they do – providing simple explanatory leaflets would help;

● improve the flow of information about and to patients/clients (especially where changes have occurred – for example, if new staff take over or new patients/clients arrive, or if there has been a change in the mental or physical state of the person, or if a history of violence is known to exist);

● improve staffing levels so as to provide the mass of personnel necessary for back-up if trouble occurs. Over-reliance on overtime working, part-timers, and poor night-cover often causes problems. Holiday and training commitments need to be taken into account when fixing establishment levels; temporary appointments may need to be expedited; there may be a need for flexible contracts so that people can move between units; there may be a need to ensure reception staff are never alone on duty; adequate reporting and recording of incidents may require more clerical staff; the reconsideration of fieldworker staffing levels may be required by the demand for doubling up on visits;

● reduce overtime and long hours since tired staff may be less able to cope with potential violence. Flexibility in the nature of appointments could be used to make it possible to switch staff around to spread the amount of hours worked more evenly and then extra cover should be provided for nights, weekends, and shift change-overs. Individuals, especially if junior, should not be isolated for long periods; backup should be readily available if an incident occurs. If the existence of a risk is established, appropriate staffing should be agreed and maintained;

● provide specialist teams to handle the most dangerous groups;

● make known the location and movements of staff so that any deviation from the planned timetable can be used as a signal that trouble may have occurred and assistance can be deployed (portable telephones for field staff make this system possible);

● provide good systems for recording incidents in order to provide an adequate basis for immediate response to the incident and for longer term strategic planning;

● have routine liaison with the police force so that they can be called in quickly. Alternatively, have your own security force on the premises (an option increasingly called for in hospitals and schools).

These recommendations have been criticized by some for reflecting a 'fortress mentality' which is antithetical to the beliefs of many practitioners. They are also costly to execute. Relatively few employers have yet put them into practice and there is little sign that more will in the near future. However, they represent one type of solution to the growing problem of violence and deserve further consideration.

POST-TRAUMA SUPPORT FOR STAFF

An example which illustrates the typical response following an assault may be useful when thinking about the role of the organization in supporting the victim.

❏ Case study: Erica

Erica, an ambulance driver, was stabbed and punched by a young man whom she had been called to transport to hospital after he had been involved in a fight outside a bar. In the fight, his opponent had held him down on the pavement and calmly chopped off two of his fingers. Erica became his target when she picked up his fingers from the floor and said that he was lucky that she had been able to find them. Erica was hospitalized overnight and released the next day with relatively minor cuts and extensive facial bruising. For the next few days, she had panic attacks whenever she had to get into a motor vehicle. She did not want to drive. After a week or so, she found that she was still not sleeping well, and when she slept she had horrific nightmares of having her face sliced into strips. She became unwilling to go outside after midday. She could not face returning to work. At odd moments, at any time, she would suddenly find herself crying. Within a month, the symptoms receded. However, for years later she would have flashbacks of the incident which were vivid in detail but pictured in monochrome.

Erica received no organizational support after the initial medical treatment. She was unaware of the probable causes for her reaction and did not have any idea what to expect next. For several weeks at the height of her reaction she was convinced that she was having a nervous breakdown. She felt intensely isolated and incapable of seeking assistance from her colleagues, many of whom felt her experience was very minor. Within four months of the incident Erica left the ambulance service. Her resignation followed an incident when she refused to respond to a call for assistance to people injured in a fight outside a bar.

Organizations employing practitioners cannot afford to leave them to cope with their own pain. The consequences for the organization can be too dangerous – alienated practitioners can be inefficient and belligerent. A positive safety culture which includes looking after your staff pays dividends in terms of efficiency and the quality of the service offered. Organizations should offer comprehensive support and counselling to victims and information on the legal assistance and compensation available to them.

Staff who have been assaulted may be suffering post-traumatic stress symptoms (see also Chapter 5). It should be added here that people vary greatly in their reactions to traumatic experiences, and they differ in the nature of the symptoms they exhibit. People also differ in the length of time it takes them to show symptoms initially and in how long symptoms persist. It is important to recognize this individual variability.

DEBRIEFING

There is growing evidence that debriefing after an assault does reduce the negative effects of the experience. There are many sorts of debriefing that vary roughly along a continuum which runs from evidence gathering to psychological assessment. *Critical-incident debriefing* involves asking:

• What happened?
• How did you feel?
• How do you feel now?

It represents an attempt to allow the person who has been assaulted to make sense of the event, perhaps together with others involved in it. This process of describing what happened and thinking through the emotions it unleashed is an important part of dispelling confusion and anxiety. It is best done soon after the event, say within 48–72 hours.

Psychological debriefing involves something closer to an attempt to provide the victim with an opportunity to explore the meaning of any emotions generated, connections with earlier life events, cognitive associations, and so on. Such debriefing sessions can be run with people who suffer PTSD symptoms several months after the event and can still have significant positive effects.

Debriefing allows the assaulted to recall details of the event, thus serving both therapeutic and organizational ends. Organizationally, it can offer vital data concerning inadequacies in any aspects of the safety procedures. The debriefing would examine in stages what happened and why, how the practitioner felt during the incident, what they feel they did wrong and what right, and what they have learned from the experience. The most important ingredient in the effective debrief is the assumption of *no-blame*. The assaulted person must feel that honesty is possible and will not result in recrimination or punishment. The no-blame norm is a central tenet of good safety cultures. Without it, people will dissemble and subvert any chance of learning useful lessons from the event.

COUNSELLING

Counselling is made available, in addition to debriefing, by some organizations as a matter of routine. The value of counselling over and above the impact of debriefing is not established. It has to be recognized that after-effects of violence may be long-term and counselling support might be needed for a long time. For practical and ethical reasons it may be best to offer counselling by some independent person, outside of the employing agency. In some social work services, external counsellors are held on retainer to provide counselling as and when events occur. Victim support and self-help schemes organized by professional groups for their own members are also being increasingly used and are thought to be valuable.

Support will usually include providing assistance to other members of the team working with the victim. They may need the opportunity to discuss the event together in a relatively structured way and may need to negotiate how they will handle both the assailant and the victim. Facilitating this may seem an obvious management task but it is one which is surprisingly frequently not done. Support for the victims may extend to enabling them to have time off work with pay beyond the period statutorily required. During this time any problems in getting back to work should be reviewed. Management should provide the victim with the option of refusing further contact with the assailant.

Management should also recognize its responsibility to the victim in opening access to any compensation scheme available for staff. Victims may be eligible for compensation as long as the incident is reported to the police. Management must also have a clear policy upon the provision of legal assistance to staff if any prosecution is pursued. Employer insurance should also be established as part of the safety policy development.

The *Assault Support Checklist* summarizes the key actions which management should be taking in response to a colleague being attacked. It is a useful aide-mémoire in the heat of dealing with the aftermath of an assault.

MANAGEMENT OF PRACTITIONER VIOLENCE

All these safeguards are directed at protecting the carer. It should also be a priority of management to safeguard those who are cared for, but this can only be achieved if management recognizes that practitioner violence occurs. Policies need to be evolved for handling practitioner violence when it surfaces. Disciplinary machinery exists

ASSAULT SUPPORT CHECKLIST

In managing the consequences of an assault you should ask yourself the following questions:

● Has debriefing been made available to all staff involved?

● Has the victim been encouraged to record all details of the event, including:

what happened;

why it happened;

how they felt during the incident;

what they thought they did wrong;

what they considered they did right;

what they learned from the incident?

● Has counselling been made available outside the victim's line-management?

● Is long-term support available if needed?

● Is the immediate line-manager alerted to check for delayed reactions?

● Have other co-workers been offered advice on how to handle the victim and (if appropriate) the assailant?

● Has practical assistance and information been made available to the victim about:

compensation schemes;

insurance schemes;

sickness leave arrangements;

prosecution of the assailant;

counselling and support services outside the employing organization;

legal assistance available from the employer?

● Has a plan been developed to enable the victim to return to work with minimal disruption and difficulty?

in all professional groups for punishing offenders. The problems lie in, firstly, identifying who they are and, secondly, in putting the machinery into action.

The costs to a profession or to an employer involved in disciplining members are very great. There is a strong likelihood that the public will generalize from the incident to other members of the profession or other employees with the consequent loss of credibility and status. The inertia of the system which results may be reinforced where practitioner violence becomes institutionalized. There are scattered reports of violence by staff in residential settings (largely adolescent treatment centres, old people's homes and hostels for the mentally handicapped). In these settings, sometimes an ethos develops in which violence by staff is acceptable and expected. The violence can be direct brutality or it can be achieved passively through long-term neglect or mistreatment. Either way, it becomes part of the culture of that institution. New staff are socialized into acceptance of it or are pressured into leaving. The problem is that this is a self-perpetuating and self-defending system. Inmates have no way of voicing complaints and staff keep silent in their own interests. The original reasons for the creation of this violent climate may disappear over time but the practices are maintained for no better reason often than habit.

Management has to face the existence of such situations. Policies need to be evolved to ensure that residential institutions can be reviewed by independent teams regularly even in the absence of any complaint. A policy of rotating staff around residential locations may also serve to break down the proclivity to violent climates.

More generally, individual practitioner violence can probably only be reduced by training programmes which enable staff to understand more of their own motivations towards violence and give them a good grasp of how and when they are most likely to become violent.

INTER-AGENCY CO-OPERATION

There is some merit in the argument that different management groups in different parts of the country should not be tackling these policy issues independently. There would be considerable advantages in imposing at least some consensual policies. Even across professional groups there is room for managerial dialogue. After all, the professions often have to act in co-operation: they could share the lessons that they are learning and they could share training activities. They could combine counselling services, all in the interests of coping with aggression more economically and comprehensively.

Beyond this there are other inter-agency obligations:

• there should be a policy on the notification of other agencies of individuals who have been violent or who are potentially violent, and there should be clear procedures on how to do so;
• there should be guidelines for the maintenance of client confidentiality under circumstances where information needs to be shared across agencies;
• joint case-management strategies may need to be developed for handling specific aggressive individuals;
• there should be comprehensive instructions to follow after a practitioner is assaulted that state which agencies should be told, under what circumstances, and with what purpose;
• other agencies should be notified of the safe-working practices which have been adopted in high-risk areas such that they can operate within your organization's constraints.

❏ Case study: Arthur

Failure to consider these obligations can result in one agency creating problems for another. For instance, the case of Arthur is instructive. Arthur was very depressed and had tried to commit suicide by taking an overdose. A social worker was asked by her team manager to take Arthur to hospital late on Friday afternoon in a car driven by Arthur's wife. They got to the hospital and Arthur's wife got out of the car and went inside. The social worker stayed in the car alone with Arthur. He suddenly realized that he was about to be admitted to the hospital, became agitated, and tried to get out of the car. The social worker leaned across to stop him and he grabbed her and started to choke her. His wife returned and stopped the incident before the social worker was badly hurt. Arthur was admitted. The social worker did not report the incident immediately since she was uninjured, the event had only lasted a moment and there was no requirement for her to do so in her agency's policy. She reported it to her line manager on Monday when she returned to work and then only in passing. In the meantime, on Friday night/early Saturday morning, Arthur assaulted a junior nurse on night duty. He tried to strangle her when she delivered his medication and she was saved from serious injury only by the intervention of another patient.

IMPROVING YOUR SAFETY CULTURE

If you are in management and you have recognized that your organization has a poor safety culture or one with specific weaknesses, it is important to try to improve it. Small, incremental changes may be feasible even where more comprehensive changes are not. It is worth re-examining your responses to the assessment exercise earlier in this chapter. Are there things which you have control over and which could be altered to improve your safety culture? If there are, consult colleagues and senior management about the direction in which you would like to go and introduce change when you get appropriate support. Remember changes in safety culture are rarely effective if imposed arbitrarily – changing culture relies upon persuasion and consent. You can change the rules and procedures and this may galvanize genuine shifts of practice in some situations but in many it will be rejected or neutralized by the informal covert safety codes which are at work.

You may not have a management position in your organization and may think it impossible for you to have an effect upon its safety culture but you can. A safety culture may be led by management but it is the product of the interaction of the activities and attitudes of all staff; everyone has a part to play in establishing good practice. You can bring to management attention problems in the safety culture. You can institute, with colleagues that work with you regularly, your own system of safety guidelines – a sort of informal safety-first network. Often grassroots developments of this sort are enormously effective in making management realize that there is a real concern among staff about an issue. A good example of this effect comes from staff-initiated counselling services for victims which sprang up initially as self-help groups but which have frequently been subsequently supported by management.

CHAPTER SUMMARY

❑ The safety culture of an organization is the product of individual and group values, attitudes, perceptions, competences, and patterns of behaviour that determine the commitment to, and the style and proficiency of, an organization's health and safety management.
❑ A positive safety culture is characterized by good two-way communication systems which result in management awareness of actual work practices and employee concerns but which ensure

everyone knows and understands safety procedures. It involves shared beliefs about the importance of safety and consensual confidence in the efficacy of the preventive measures in operation.

❑ Management in the caring professions has a vital role to play in coping with aggression. There is a process for managing safety which involves setting clear policy, creating organizational structures to implement policy, erecting safety standards, assessing compliance with these standards, imposing operational controls to help execution of the policy, continuous monitoring of performance of staff, and systematic review of measures at regular intervals.

❑ Organizational strategies for coping with aggression should include: guidelines for practice; training programmes; modification of the working environment; post-trauma support for staff; management of practitioner violence; and inter-agency co-operation.

❑ Everyone has a role to play in maintaining and improving safety culture.

Chapter Eight

Sensitization and Realism

INTERPRETABLE AGGRESSION

The main purpose of this book is to sensitize you to what is known about acts of aggression against practitioners and to help you to make a realistic estimate of the risks you face and acquire a repertoire of strategies for coping with them. While the focus has been upon carers at work, many of the lessons will transfer into other types of interaction at home and at leisure. The clues to risk are less well-documented in domestic or leisure contexts, mainly because the situations involved are too varied, but the skills for coping with aggression are similar. Tactics for de-escalation and escape are useful *wherever* you face aggression.

It is important to recognize that you are unlikely to be able to use these tactics if you treat aggression as uninterpretable. The Assault Cycle is not peculiar to exchanges between practitioners and clients, it is common to *all* violent exchanges. It offers a framework for interpreting *any* aggression that you experience. The social psychological theories which explain the initiation of aggression and victimization of the assaulted are applicable to all incidents. The descriptions of the stages in post-assault reactions apply to all victims. Aggression and its effects become interpretable against the background of such explanations.

SUMMARY OF THE KEY PRINCIPLES IN COPING WITH AGGRESSIVE BEHAVIOUR

Coping with aggressive behaviour is not simply a matter of dealing with the immediate demands of an incident. It involves the whole process of preparing yourself for the possibility of violence, handling the incident, and responding to its aftermath. The underlying principles which should guide your actions when dealing with aggression, whether at work or elsewhere, can be summarized as follows:

- Always be aware of the indicators of risk;

- Always consciously make a risk estimate before engaging in any encounter that entails any sort of risk of aggression;

- Respond early to any indications that there will be violence – do not doubt your own fears, do not ignore warning signs (especially not verbal threats or abuse);

- Choose avoidance or evasion rather than confrontation;

- Use de-escalation tactics and refuse to get caught up in retaliation;

- Manage your own anxiety so as to maximize your chances of remaining calm and in control of your own thoughts and actions;

- Rehearse your repertoire of coping tactics until they are habits and come quickly and 'naturally' without you feeling that you have to think what to do;

- Rid yourself of stereotypes concerning the victims of assault;

- Be aware of the short- and long-term consequences for yourself and the assailant of involvement in aggressive incidents of varying levels of severity;

- Be aware of the support available to you in dealing with an aggressive situation or in coping with the after-effects of involvement in one;

- Report incidents;

- Use debriefing after an incident;

- Be alert to the possibility that other people (colleagues or family) may be suffering the after-effects of involvement in an incident and be ready to help them;

- Know your own preferences for different forms of aggression and be aware of the triggers which precipitate you into violence;

- Be proactive in removing or minimizing the triggers which engender violence;

- Be realistic about your own abilities and the way you respond.

Keeping to these principles is not easy and they require the acquisition of a wide variety of analytical and interpersonal skills. The collation and interpretation of information in order to calculate risks realistically entails quite sophisticated analytical methods; consequently, it is sensible to use any prefabricated method (such as the *Dangerousness Checklist*) if it is available. Of course, for domestic and leisure incidents such shortcuts are not available. The interpersonal abilities needed fundamentally revolve around communication skills. You need to be able to communicate to potential assailants that:

- you recognize and accurately understand their feelings and thoughts;
- you respect their rights and concerns;
- you are competent and confident;
- you are calm;
- you know what you want them to do and can be specific in instructions.

You may also need to be able to communicate a range of sentiments (fear, anger, remorse, and so on). The essential skill lies in being able to communicate the emotion which you wish to transmit, rather than something you want to hide (for example, pride, disgust). Controlling what you communicate in the midst of aggression is not easy. It takes much practice. If offered the opportunity, you should use role plays in training to practise communicating different types of emotional message whilst you are in a highly aroused condition. You may well find that the emotions which get transmitted are quite different from the ones you want to emit. Repeated practice will help you to acquire control.

It is worth noting that it is not so much what you say as the way you say it which carries messages about your emotional state. People who are in a highly aroused state are particularly sensitive to the non-verbal aspects of communication. These include body posture and eye contact but also include the non-verbal aspects of vocalization. For instance, they include tone, speed of speech, breathlessness, hesitancies, and so on. These are the clues to your emotional state. People are not consistent in how they interpret these cues, but it is worth considering whether these aspects of how you say what you say are telltale clues to your underlying fear or doubt. An assailant will hear this message if it is present. You should work on controlling this part of how you communicate.

Most people also need organizational support to become better in coping with aggression. Individual skills are important but organizational safety culture is vital when considering dealing with aggression at work. If you do not have a good organizational safety culture now, you should try to get one developed. Organizations have obligations for the safety of their staff which they cannot afford to ignore, and as an individual employee you can militate for improvements in safety culture. You have the right to do so. A key principle for coping with aggression which should be added to the list is: insist that your employer supports a safety culture that serves to protect you. The single most useful thing an employer can do is to introduce a 'no-blame' policy.

In large part, the knowledge gained after reading this book should be self-knowledge, both for practitioners and their managers. Practitioners should have a greater appreciation of the nature and extent of violence and aggression in both their work and non-work lives. They should have a better idea of the forms of violence which they prefer to exhibit and they should be aware of the characteristics of the most likely assailants and be able to use the *Dangerousness Checklist* in order to assess the risk involved in a contact. They should have mentally rehearsed the strategies they feel they would personally be able to use if faced with an attack situation. They should have explored the value of assertiveness techniques and anxiety management procedures. They should be aware of the likely pattern of reactions in the victim after an assault and how other professionals and society more broadly stereotype the victim.

Managers should know the level of risk faced by their staff and have reviewed whether they have actually fulfilled their functions with regard to establishing procedural guidelines, supporting staff, structuring training, and providing safeguards. The caring professions will only be able to face violence effectively when both practitioners and their managers act in concert upon the knowledge they possess. They should do everything they can to improve, and then use, their knowledge of the aetiology, ecology, and natural history of aggression and violence.

REFERENCES

Bandura, A. (1969). *Principles of Behaviour Modification*. New York: Rinehart & Winston.

Berkowitz, L. (Ed.) (1969). *Roots of Aggression: A Re-examination of the Frustration–Aggression Hypothesis*. New York: Atherton.

Berkowitz, L. (Ed.) (1994). On the escalation of aggression. In M. Potegal and J.F. Knutson (Eds) *The Dynamics of Aggression*. Hillsdale, USA: Lawrence Erlbaum.

Brown, R., Bute, S., and Ford, P. (1986). *Social Workers at Risk: The Prevention and Management of Violence*. London: MacMillan.

Collins, J.J. (1990). Summary thoughts about drugs and violence. *National Institute on Drug Abuse Research Monograph Series, 103,* 265–275.

Collins, J.J. and Messerschmidt, P.M. (1993). Epidemiology of alcohol-related violence. Special Issue: Alcohol, aggression and injury. *Alcohol Health and Research World, 17(2),* 93–100.

Coontz, P.D., Lidz, C.W., and Mulvey, E.P. (1994). Gender and the assessment of dangerousness in the Psychiatric Emergency Room. *International Journal of Law and Psychiatry, 17(4),* 369–376.

Cox, S., and Cox, T. (1991). The structure of employee attitudes to safety: A European example. *Work and Stress, 5 (2),* 93–106.

Crane, D. (1986). *Violence on Social Workers*. University of East Anglia Social Work Monograph 46.

Dollard, J., Doob, L.W., Miller, N.E., Mowrer, O.H., and Sears, R.H. (1939). *Frustration and Aggression*. New Haven, Conn: Yale University Press.

Durkin, K. (1995). *Developmental Social Psychology*. Oxford: Blackwell.

Farrington, D. (1987). Early Precursors of Frequent Offending. In J. Q. Wilson and G. C. Loury (Eds) *From Children to Citizens Vol III*. New York: Springer-Verlag.

Flannery, R.B. (1995). *Violence in the Workplace*. New York, USA: Crossroad Pub.Co.

Gardner, J. and Gray, M. (1982). Violence Towards Children. In P. Feldman (Ed.) *Developments in the Study of Criminal Behaviour Vol.2*. Chichester: Wiley.

Giancola, P. and Zeichner, A. (1995). Alcohol-related aggression in males and females. *Alcoholism Clinical and Experimental Research, 19(1),* 130–134.

Goldstein, P.J. (1985). The drugs/violence nexus: a tripartite conceptual framework. *Journal of Drug Issues, 15(4),* 493–506.

Gustafson, R. (1994). Alcohol and aggression. *Journal of Offender Rehabilitation, 21(3–4)*, 41–80.

Janis, I.L. (1976). Groupthink. In E. Hollander and R. Hunt (Eds) *Current Perspectives in Social Psychology*. Oxford: Oxford University Press.

Kahneman, D., Slovic, P., and Tversky, A. (1982). *Judgement Under Uncertainty: Heuristics and Biases*. New York: Cambridge University Press.

McBride, D.C. and Scharter, J.A. (1990). Drugs and violence in the age of crack cocaine. In: R.A. Weisheit (Ed.) *Drugs, crime and the criminal justice system*. Cincinnati, USA: Anderson Pub.Co.

McPhail, C. (1994). The dark side of purpose: individual and collective violence in riots. *Sociological Quarterly, 35(1)*, 1–32.

Moore, B.E. (Ed) (1995) *Psychoanalysis: The major concepts*. New Haven, CT: Yale University Press.

Owens, R. G. and Ashcroft, J. B. (1985) *Violence: A Guide for the Caring Professions*. London: Croom Helm.

Prentice-Dunn, S. (1990). Perspectives on research classics: Two routes to collective violence. *Contemporary Social Psychology, 14(4)*, 217–218.

Rowett, C. (1986). Violence in Social Work. *Institute of Criminology Occasional Paper No 14*, Cambridge University.

Scheidlinger, S. (1994). A commentary on adolescent group violence. *Child Psychiatry and Human Development, 25(1)*, 3–11.

Staub, E. (1991). The psychological and cultural roots of group violence. *Journal of Psychohistory, 19(1)*, 115–121.

Webster, C.D., Harris, G.T., Rice, M.E., Cormier, C., and Quinsey, V.L. (1994). *The Violence Prediction Scheme: Assessing dangerousness in high risk men*. Burnaby, BC, Canada: Simon Fraser University.

Weiner, B. (1995). *Judgments of Responsibility*. New York, USA: Guilford Press.

Weisman, A.M. and Taylor, S.P. (1994). Effect of alcohol and risk of physical harm on human physical aggression. *Journal of General Psychology, 121(1)*, 67–75.

Winkel, F.-W. and Denkers, A. (1995). Crime victims and their social network: A field study on the cognitive effects of victimisation, attributional responses and the victim-blaming model. *International Review of Victimology, 3(4)*, 309–322.

FURTHER READING

Bandura, A. (1973). *Aggression: A Social Learning Analysis.* Englewood Cliffs, NJ: Prentice Hall.

Baron, R.A. and Richardson, D.T. (1994). *Human Aggression (2nd Edition).* New York: Plenum.

Berkowitz, L. (1986). *A Survey of Social Psychology.* New York: Holt, Rinehart & Winston.

Breakwell, G.M. (1989). *Facing Physical Violence.* Leicester: BPS Books and Routledge. Now out of print.

Breakwell, G.M. and Rowett, C. (1989). Violence and Social Work. In J. Archer and K. Browne (Eds) *Human Aggression: Naturalistic Approaches.* London: Routledge.

Brewer, J.D. (1994). *The Dangers From Strangers: Confronting the Threat of Assault.* New York: Plenum.

Finney, G. (1988). One False Move. *Community Outlook,* April.

Freud, S. (1930). *Civilisation and Its Discontents.* London: Hogarth Press.

Gorer, G. (1968). Man has no 'killer' instinct. In M.F.A. Montague (Ed.) *Man and Aggression.* New York: Oxford University Press.

Health Services Advisory Committee (1987). *Violence to Staff in the Health Services.* London: Health and Safety Executive, HMSO.

Houghton, S., Wheldall, K., and Merrett, F. (1988). Classroom behaviour problems which secondary school teachers say they find most troublesome. *British Education Research Journal, 14(3),* 295–310.

Huesmann, L.R. (Ed.) (1994). *Aggressive Behaviour.* New York: Plenum.

Kaplan, S.G. and Wheeler, E.G. (1983). Survival skills for working with potentially violent clients. *Social Casework, 64,* 339–346.

Kidd, B. and Stark, C. (Eds) (1995). *Managements of Violence and Aggression in Health Care.* London: Gaskell.

Lorenz, K. (1966). *On Aggression.* New York: Harcourt, Brace & World.

Marsh, P. and Campbell, A. (Eds) (1982). *Aggression and Violence.* Oxford: Blackwell.

Montagu, A. (1976). *The Nature of Human Aggression.* New York: Oxford University Press.

Mullender, A. (1995). *The Handbook of Domestic Violence.* London: Routledge.

Parker, C. and Etherington, S. (1984). *Out of Hours Social Work.* London: British Association of Social Workers.

Poyner, B. and Warne, C. (1985). *Violence to Staff: A Basis for Assessment and Prevention* HMSO, London.

Rowett, C. and Breakwell, G.M. (1992). *Managing Violence at Work.* Slough: NFER-Nelson.

Scott, R.L. (1977). Communications as an intentional, social system. *Human Communication Research, 3,* 35–54.

Siann, G. (1985). *Accounting for Aggression: Perspectives on aggression and violence.* Boston: Allen & Unwin.

Straus, M.A., Gelles, R.J., and Steinmetz, S.K. (1980). *Behind Closed Doors: Violence in the American family.* New York: Doubleday.

Tutt, N. (Ed.) (1976). *Violence.* London: HMSO.

Wilson, E.O. (1975). *Sociobiology: The new synthesis.* Boston, Mass.: Harvard University Press.

INDEX:

Compiled by Frances Coogan